LOVE
BETWEEN
EQUALS

LOVE BETWEEN EQUALS

How Peer Marriage Really Works

PEPPER SCHWARTZ, Ph.D.

FP

THE FREE PRESS

New York   London   Toronto   Sydney   Tokyo   Singapore

The Free Press
A Division of Simon & Schuster, Inc.
1230 Avenue of the Americas, New York, N.Y. 10020

First Free Press Paperback Edition 1995

Printed in the United States of America

printing number

1 2 3 4 5 6 7 8 9 10

Library of Congress Cataloging-in-Publication Data

Schwartz, Pepper.
  [Peer marriage]
Love between equals: how peer marriage really works / Pepper
  Schwartz.—1st Free Press Paperback ed.
      p.   cm.
  ISBN 0-02-874061-0 (pbk.)
  1. Marriage—United States.   2. Sex role—United States.
I. Title.
HQ536.S394   1995
306.81—dc20   95–13617
                                                           CIP

To the memory of Philip Blumstein,
dearest friend, muse, and collaborator

And to Art, Cooper, and Ryder—my peer team

Contents

Acknowledgments

First, my gratitude and sad farewell to Philip Blumstein. Phil and I envisioned and began this project together. We only parted ways on it because he was struck down by AIDS. He was my colleague in the University of Washington Sociology Department, writing partner and dear friend for twenty years. I also write this greatly missing Gerry Jordan, Philip's partner and my close friend. He too is gone, a victim of the AIDS epidemic. Gerry and Phil's relationship was a peer marriage and a model of love and devotion.

As to the living, thanks to Jane Adams, wonderful writer and encouraging friend who helped with several proposals and was always just the right person to bounce ideas off of; Peter Davison, poet and editor, who gave me great help crafting a model chapter; Lynn Nesbitt and her agency, who worked hard for an earlier incarnation of this book; Joseph Troxel, secretary extraordinaire, Karen Tye, my smart, absolutely dependable right-hand woman who does everything from type, deftly read editorial comments that defy others' decoding, search for cites and in short, works tirelessly for however long it takes to get things done; Claire Rabin, for many discussions on this topic—and almost a collaboration; Bruce Nichols, my absolutely wonderful, wise, and enthusiastic editor who sought this book and who never has been anything less than stalwart in its protection, correction, and advancement. What a pleasure he has been to work with, talk with, think with. May all writers be so fortunate!

Thanks also to the Sociology Department at the University of Washington, which gave secretarial and moral support, especially the unflagging good humor and aid of Myrna Torries in the front office. And to my friends and colleagues at KIRO-TV for the on-the-job training I receive there correcting academic mangling of English (and apologies for my occasional backsliding). Most importantly, a thank you to my wonderful children Cooper and Ryder and my terrific friends, on both coasts and in between; they give me all the love and understanding anyone could ever ask for—especially when I test them by disappearing under a writing frenzy. And in a special category, my husband Art—for fourteen years of love and friendship with just the right amount of collaboration and freedom. Our peer marriage made this book on peer marriage possible. And last, but not in any way least, a huge thank you for all the couples—peer or not—who told me about their most private thoughts and acts. Thank you for your trust, generosity and truth. Thank you for giving your stories to me—and to the readers of this book.

PEER
MARRIAGE

— *Chapter 1* —

The Hard Experience
of Equality

I n 1983 Philip Blumstein and I published the results of a large
study on the nature of American relationships; it was called *American Couples*. The study, which received an enormous amount of
notice from the press and the public, was composed of over 12,000
questionnaires and 600 interviews from married, cohabiting, lesbian,
and gay members of couples.[1] During the course of what turned out
to be a decade-long effort, I noticed that there were many same-sex
couples with an egalitarian relationship but very few such heterosexual couples. Because the homosexual couples did not have to surmount the traditions of sex differences, they more often worked out
relationships that both partners felt were fair and supportive to each
other. My curiosity about their success at this aspect of their relationship, plus my admiration for the few egalitarian heterosexual couples
in the study, made me want to know more about how married couples
could get past traditions of gender and construct a relationship built
on equality. Previous sociological studies on marriage made chances
for egalitarian marriage seem grim, but since my own marriage was
successfully egalitarian, I had both scientific and personal motivation

1

to see why some couples reconstructed gender roles and others did not. To that end, I reexamined some of the egalitarian marriages in the *American Couples* study, used them as an archetype, and then sought more of these couples to talk to and learn from.

The couples, I discovered, based their marriages on a mix of equity (each person gives in proportion to what he or she receives) and equality (each person has equal status and is equally responsible for emotional, economic, and household duties). But these couples were distinguished by more than their dedication to fairness and collaboration; the most happy and durable among them also had refocused their relationship on *intense companionship*. To be sure, they shared child raising, chores, and decision making more or less equally and almost always equitably, but for most of them, this was just part of a plan for a true companionship marriage. The point of the marriage was not to share everything fifty-fifty. Rather, the shared decisions, responsibility, and household labor were in the service of an intimate and deeply collaborative marriage. I call this kind of marriage peer marriage; it is a marriage of equal companions, a collaboration of love and labor in order to produce profound intimacy and mutual respect.

The people in peer marriage for the most part are not ideologues. They construct and maintain a peer marriage because they find it rewarding. If they are without the means to hire the services of a homemaker, they seek work that allows both spouses to share child care and housework. These couples do not strike acquaintances as odd; they look just like their friends and co-workers, except that they have vigilantly preserved their commitment to equality. Additionally, they see peer marriage as salvation from instability. Many of them have witnessed the deterioration of their own previous marriage, or that of friends, and they believe that the only way to maintain a lifetime together is to create an irreplaceable, and interdependent, union of equals.

This book examines these people. I compare examples from this small but provocative group to traditional couples—those who divide male and female roles into separate spheres of influence and responsibility, with final authority given to the husband—and to couples I call "near peers"—those who admire egalitarian relations between men and women but cannot figure out how to do it. Both partners in a near-peer relationship are likely to work and to believe in female equality, but the woman does much more child care and the man usually has veto power in a way the woman does not. Much of the Western world fits the near-peer description, and we know a lot about them. What we need now is an analysis of those couples who have made it to the other side. The book is meant for all couples who seek a truly satisfying relationship and are willing to think about equality as the road to that kind of marriage.

This book is *not* simplistic cheerleading in favor of equality in marriage. We assess the costs as well as the benefits of equality. Some readers may be men and women who tried equality but failed but might try again if they thought it could be done more successfully. Many readers may be members of couples starting out, who are looking for a model to follow but recognizing the obstacles to constructing an egalitarian relationship. The book will also help unhappy traditional couples who are suffering from the effects of inequality, though they may only suspect that it is the source of their problems.

This study argues that traditional couples sacrifice the elemental goals of intimacy, deep friendship, and (whether they know it or not) mutual respect, goals that peer marriage better serves. I also found that peers face new problems: They may have tamer, perhaps less intense sex lives; they enjoy fewer external sources of validation; they may be so close that they exclude others; figuring out the right mix of equity and equality is difficult and emotionally taxing; and they cannot as easily pursue their careers to the fullest extent possible.

When I was first looking for egalitarian couples to interview about their relationship, most men and women responded by asking "Are there any?" Although I can emphatically answer yes, it is certainly true that peer couples are hardly the majority form of marriage, and few researchers have sought to find the ones who do exist. Almost everything that has been printed on marriage has been on the impossibility of equality and the additional burdens brought on by women's entry into the labor force. Arlie Hochschild's thoughtful book, *The Second Shift*, is a powerful statement to women about how they remain unliberated from traditional roles and responsibilities.[2] I do not deny that the number of couples who share power and divide their emotional duties and household tasks equitably is small, but it can be done, and the rewards of this reshuffling of traditional gender relations are significant: a deep and true partnership based on equality, equity, and intimacy.

For this book, I used a much smaller sample of couples than my coauthor and I did in *American Couples*, but I build on the same interview technique: approximately two-hour interviews held separately with each spouse (in this study, on different evenings) and then a joint interview of about an hour to an hour and a half. The couples were gathered via two routes. First, about thirty were contacted from the *American Couples* pool. After they were interviewed, they were asked if they "knew anyone else like themselves." Friends, acquaintances, and friends of friends in six different cities (Seattle, San Francisco, New York, Chicago, Los Angeles, and Washington, D.C.) were located and interviewed. This is hardly a representative sample, but the couples were not chosen to represent a random sample of marriages, even of "liberal" marriages. Rather, they were chosen precisely because they were unusual; they shared traditional male and female tasks, organized their relationship on the principles of equity and equality, and avoided traditional hierarchy between males and females.

There was an element of "I can't define it, but I know it when I see it" to my initial search. There is certainly more than one way of conceptualizing fairness. It is theoretically possible for couples to be equitable within certain traditional role division (and indeed some of the peers in this book are single-career couples), but when couples organize their marriage according to traditional male breadwinner–female household manager and mother roles, it is very difficult psychologically to separate rhetoric about equality (each of us has dignity and equality in our sphere) from reality (he really does not think housecleaning is as important as what he does because he would never do it himself). Almost all the research on couples who have separate spheres of influence find that these partners do not share equal power. In this study, among the couples in which the mother did not work outside the home, both partners deviated from the traditional pattern in all other respects.

In general, four characteristics of peer couples emerged. First, the partners did not generally have more than a sixty-forty traditional split of household duties and child raising. (An exception was made for the early periods of infancy, and even then, there had to be significant paternal involvement.) Second, each partner believed that each person in the couple had equal influence over important and disputed decisions. Third, partners felt that they had equal control over the family economy and reasonably equal access to discretionary funds. Most research has indicated that money confers power and relative income influences decision making.[3] These couples either had to earn similar amounts, or share power over family resources (such as having similar ability to undertake nonmonitored private spending). Fourth, each person's work was given equal weight in the couple's life plans. The person with the less glamorous and remunerative job could not always be the person with the most housework or child care. The requirement of sharing money, influence, decision making, child care and homemaking applied even for couples in which one person had a salaried job and the other stayed home. Among older couples, a history of traditional role division that no longer existed was allowable as long as it had not been true for the previous three years. The point was not to define these characteristics as the only way to reach a just, rewarding, and durable relationship but to use them to define the new, and spreading, phenomenon of marriages in which traditional roles were absent and there was no hidden hierarchy.

The peer marriages I identified were then compared to traditional and near-peer couples, who were more or less congruent on age, duration of relationship, and class. Partners were asked, separately and together, about their previous relationships, the history of their marriage, the evolution of their egalitarian feelings and behaviors, and descriptions of how they handled communication, conflict, sex and intimacy, money, children, job and other life-style issues.

My snowball sample (the term sociologists use for a sample whereby one person recommends the next) makes any statistical conclusions about peer couples seriously suspect. Nonetheless, certain attributes appeared again and again and are at least worth mentioning, if only as a guide for future research. These couples tended to be dual income; only three couples contained women who did not work at all. They were in their late twenties to mid-forties. There was only one much older couple (in their mid-sixties) and only a few in their mid-fifties. The age similarity was partially an artifact of the snowball sample but also probably a cohort effect. It was the baby boom generation who came of age at a time when feminist ideology was having its rebirth. This generation, born between 1945 and 1957, and its younger followers had to evaluate whether to embrace the new tenets and criticisms of marriage, or opt for the traditional model. The baby boom and post–baby boom women who endorsed feminist philosophy—or at least wanted to shuck old gender roles and constraints—have had to consider consciously the role of marriage in determining their life. Some had to think about *if* they wanted to be married, and all have examined *how* they wanted to be married. More of these women might be expected to want a relationship that gives them equal standing in marriage. Oddly, younger women among this group sometimes assumed a certain amount of equality and equity and thereby unconsciously settled for less.

This cohort explanation may also explain why almost half of these marriages contain a previously divorced partner. People in this age group have a higher divorce rate than the cohorts ahead of them. Also, the older women of the baby boom generation were more likely to have started marriage under one set of norms and reexamined it under a new, more feminist consciousness. Most of these women who were previously divorced said they left their first marriage because of inequitable treatment. Peer men were far more likely to recite a great number of reasons for the breakup of their marriage but were also likely to say it was either the end of their marriage or the difficult period after the marriage was over, a devastating period of fighting over property and support, that made them seek a peer relationship. Accusations of betrayal or continued emotional and financial dependence of the ex-spouse made these men much more interested in a different kind of marriage the next time: an independent, working spouse who could hold her own in a partnership.

The last, and rather unexpected, commonality among the peer couples was that they tended to be more middle class than working or upper middle class. As we shall see, egalitarian couples seem more likely when male income is not so grand that it encourages a non-working wife or makes the wife's income unimportant. When a peer marriage had a high-earning male, it was likely there was also a high-earning female (or, as in a couple of cases, a female with a prestigious job such as an elected politician or a successful artist). But generally, most male occupations were *not* high pressure and high profile. It seems to be easier to create an egalitarian relationship if the man has a job (or creates one) that has some flexibility and controllable hours, and if both partners make similar amounts of money (for example, if both partners are teachers). Still, these kinds of background data do not provide the answers to the most intriguing commonalities of all: How did these people come to be in an egalitarian marriage? Why did they want to be peers?

Why Peer Marriage?

To any woman who was or is part of the women's movement, the answer to this question is clear. Women in the recent history of the United States, Canada, and most of Western European have experienced a rise in personal freedom that can be expected to extend to their family and personal life. This is particularly true for the women of the baby boom generation who grew up indulged by a kind economy and relatively permissive parents and who, along with the males in their cohort, rebelled against traditional social expectations: what it meant to be a women, a man, a partner, a spouse.

Their critique of traditional marriage included the perception that it was unacceptably anti-individualistic. Traditionally, marriage is a corporate entity in which the self is supposed to be transformed to fulfill, depending on one's gender, the demands of supporter and provider, or father and mother. Both men and women, but especially a number of women, defied that loss of individuality and rigid description of duties. Women, for example, decided, either rationally or de facto, that virginity was no longer required in order to be a desirable spouse or a good wife. The institutionalization of premarital sex was just part of the questioning of gender requirements. Young people proclaimed that individual happiness was more important than familial duty. There was a general rejection of capitulation to traditional expectations. A number of women wrote about new ways to be female. Theories of male oppression and patriarchal culture flourished. And although the number of women who directly participated in these forums may have been statistically small, the reach of their thoughts and feelings was deep and broad. Women left marriage—or were left—in extraordinary numbers, the divorce rate has more than doubled since the early 1960s. Both women who stayed in marriages and women who left them learned a new language of anger and inequity. The appetite for equality and equity grew nationally and internationally, and even those who held on to traditional values about roles and relationships found themselves more aware and critical of some of the bargains of male and female relations.

This history of marital change is widely known. The women's movement made women aware that they did not have a fair deal in most spheres of their life, and they started to demand more standing and more ability to set some of the terms of their intimate relationships. Men resisted some of these demands, but, particularly after the 1970s, there was a wide agreement that relationships should be more equal, fairer, and less separated by sex role distinctions. The surprise is not that marriage should change; rather, it is that *more* change has not happened, that most marriages remain hierarchical. The reason, surely, is not that women like to take orders or believe in male omnipotence. Women have been too much in the world to accept heavy-handed subordination; the mystique of men has been watered down by the dialogue of the women's movement and the discussion of male shortcomings in the mass media; and women have found, by choice and by necessity, that they too can be achievers in the work world. There is still both perceived and real impediment to high earnings for women, but there are also widely known success stories of women who have proved themselves every bit as talented and entrepreneurial as men. Even small towns now have women's business networks, women in Rotary and other leadership organizations, women mayors, women principals, and so forth.

Nevertheless, some social forces and psychological processes tenaciously maintain marriage along the old guidelines. Women still look to men to provide life-style and to create the larger and more predictable income that establishes the family's social class and creature comforts. The idea of equal economic responsibility is one that neither sex feels entirely comfortable with, and although job mobility has opened up for women, many still view the world of work as daunting, and preferably optional.

The fruits of male income are a serious impediment to the reconstruction of couple interaction. As long as it seems (and is) easier for men to make a better living than women, both men and women can comfortably allow male job requirements to drive the rest of family functioning. This is done in a rather egalitarian fashion at first. Newlyweds believe that they can put together a "separate but equal" marriage, with each taking care of traditional male and female tasks but with overall influence in the marriage being equal. Empirical observation of these arrangements does not bear this theory out. The buck tends to stop at the desk of the person who made it, and over time the husband feels he has more right to allocate its dispersal and impact.

Territorialization—the taking and governing of separate spheres of interest—spreads when children arrive. As long as the woman accepts child raising as her responsibility, she gains power in this area but loses the ability to expect major investment of male parenting time. Both husbands and wives are loathe to jeopardize male earning capacity in the service of child raising, and even if they would like to involve the father more, the work world conspires to make it difficult. Employers may give lip-service to the importance of the family but for the most part will not reward a man who asks for a customized schedule so that he can be a good father. The lionization of active fatherhood is not enough of a reward to most fathers when the economic costs of equality in parenting are so obvious. As a result, women lavish praise on husbands who spend any of time with their children, and men learn that they get heavily rewarded for even minor shows of parental solidarity. Over time, the separation of male and female parenting duties becomes solidified, and couples feel that the division of labor over child care is inevitable.

These serious economic barriers to equality are matched by psychological barriers. Centuries of hierarchical relationships between men and women have made that arrangement seem natural. Men have been trained to lead, women to lean. Male leadership is lauded as one of the definitive aspects of masculinity; femininity is supposed to be vulnerable and supportive. Even in nominally equal relationships, wives still take some pleasure in deferring to a forceful husband, and husbands take pride in unambiguously claiming the position of head of household. Although modern men are much more likely to want a wife who contributes to family income and who is a "person in her own right," they still feel some nervousness when women ask for equal status in the household. All human beings like to get their own way, but men have enjoyed that privilege as a right and expectation. So males support female equality but only up to the point it collides with their privilege. At that time, they invoke either a theory of leadership or a theory of cooperation, both of which include female capitulation on items that depend on male economic providership. Men may speak about equality, but they fight it when their hold on hierarchy becomes tenuous. Small symbolic acts make the point: Women cannot lead when they dance with men; large purchases, like a car, are rarely made by women on their own.

Previous traditions have been modified but not dislodged because, at base, there is a real fear not just of change but of *revolution*. There is almost a terror that men will no longer be men and women will no longer be women. The not-so-hidden belief of many men and women is that there are fundamental arrangements of male-female connection, and they are not to be tinkered with.

Of course, even if we wanted to, we could not erase all the differences between men and women that make them attracted and attached to each other, emotionally, erotically, and pragmatically. But now that we offer a real possibility of equality, many people get cold feet. They do not seek true equality because they are scared that all they will get is trouble for their effort. In some ways, the most dangerous impact of well-meaning books like *The Second Shift* is that they confirm readers' worst fears about the changing nature of male and female roles: that liberated women will only be liberated for more work, less love, less protection, and more exploitation. Men and women are worried about who they will have to be if they give up their traditional gender territories and remap their personal and family life. They are worried as well that the opening up of roles to personal choice rather than by sex will obliterate sexual differences and the interdependence of the sexes. Men and women know how to enjoy gender and marriage by the old ways, they feel lost when it comes to egalitarian marriage, have trouble believing the rewards of peer marriage would be worth the sacrifice it takes to get there, and they feel they are good enough where they are, having made significant strides from their parents' marriages and moving as close to egalitarian as they will ever get. They don't believe they can take the next step, so they stop short of it. They have a false sense of how far they have come and how far it is possible to go, they do not realize that the path they are on is not actually leading them to the place they want to go.

Then why peer marriage? Why have some couples moved through this considerable gauntlet to create an egalitarian partnership? Most simply, it is because they want to love each other as much as possible. They want a marriage that has intensity and partnership and does not create the distance between men and women that is inevitable between people of unequal status and power. These men and women looked at the lack of intimacy, and even at the anger and resentment between their parents or in previous relationships of their own, and wanted to avoid replication. Women who were consciously feminist did not want to be angry about inequity; men in love did not want to have an accusatory and resentful partner. Men and women who began as friends became deeply committed to maintaining that friendship, and took steps to preserve the relationship from the impact of traditional marriage. The common theme among these peer couples is the preservation of intimacy, the desire to be neither oppressor nor oppressed, the commitment to a relationship that creates a shared universe rather than parallel lives. When they designed their relationship to ensure those goals, the rewards of peer marriage became self-reinforcing.

But Who Would Be a Peer Man?

The common perception is that men do not want a peer marriage. Why should they give up all the privileges conferred by traditional marriage? And even if we can imagine that a man would like to share the burden of supporting a family or would like a career woman with whom to share his life, we know that most men have been loath to take on the burdens that women carry. It is hard to imagine as well that men who have the opportunity for high earnings and a prestigious job would sacrifice either for a more participatory family life. Because of these and similar observations, many women feel that peer men are born, not made, and so few of them exist that they are not worth looking for.

That is a misconception. Peer men often *are* made, *not* born. Many men came to peer values after they tried a fairly traditional relationship and found it didn't work for them. The enjoyed having service, support and household management from a traditional wife or a girlfriend—up to a point. Then they reported being either bored or overwhelmed with responsibility. Some fell in love with a "new woman"—an independent peer who was exactly the sort of woman they avoided or felt insecure around when they were younger. Many of the first wives of these men were furious at losing husbands after they had fulfilled the contract they both had signed. And when these women dated or remarried, they no longer presented themselves as they had as younger, more traditional women.

Others of these men had had traditional relationships that they liked just the way they were, until they went sour for a variety of reasons. It was the aftermath of the separation, divorce, custody, and alimony battles that changed their mind about what they wanted in their next relationship. Many of these men were very attached to their children and vowed never again to be the minor parent. Others had ex-wives who were lost without them, and the responsibility and guilt of that situation made them look for someone stronger.

Nevertheless, some of these men *were* "born peer." They came from homes where they got along with and respected an impressive mother or sister. Some had grown up doing their fair share of chores and babysitting. Quite a few of them were men who never felt comfortable with macho standards of masculinity. They liked female company; they liked to talk; they liked being in a family environment. One common distinguishing factor is that they liked children, looked forward to having their own, and wanted to be involved in the day-to-day upbringing of their family.

Some of these men were ambitious in their work; others were clear from the beginning that their work would come second to their marriage and family. But what they usually shared in common was the idea that they wanted an in-depth personal relationship that would not be sacrificed to work. They wanted a best friend.

It was this goal of deeper friendship that helped to "make" peer men. Much of what evolved between these men and women happened because of their strong desire to stay emotionally connected to one another. They saw each other as individuals rather than as roles and wanted the same things for each other that they sought for themselves. More often than not, the women in these relationships were good communicators and were clear about how they wanted and needed to be treated; they had a strong sense of what was a fair deal. The men had the ability to understand and support their partner's wishes. Most of these couples had to negotiate early in the relationship—and keep negotiating throughout it—to keep it a partnership rather than watching it slip into more traditional roles. One of the interesting things about peer men, is that they too had an investment in keeping that from happening. They were looking for an equal, a partner and a friend. They didn't want to lose that person to pressures to live a more conventional relationship.

My impression is that many of the near peer men I interviewed could have been peers if their wives had insisted on it and the men and the women had resisted the pressures that his job put on their family. The difference between peer men and near-peer men was one of degree rather than a differential desire or individual psychological capability. The peer men were more committed to their goals of partnership and participation or had partners who kept them from slipping into the more familiar and easier-to-manage traditional roles. The combination of a man and woman working *together* to have a peer marriage ultimately made their partnership possible, stable, and rewarding.

Rewards of Peer Marriage

Primacy of the Relationship

Egalitarian couples give priority to their relationship over their work and over all other relationships—with friends, extended family, even their children. Their mutual friendship is the most satisfying part of their lives. The point of equality and equity in these relationships is to create a marriage that makes each partner feel secure in the other person's regard and support.

Intimacy

Peer couples experience much more of each other's lives than do traditional or near peers. Because they share housework, children, and economic responsibility, they empathize as well as sympathize. They experience the world in a more similar way, understand the other partner's personality more accurately, and communicate better because they know each other and each other's world better and because equal power in the relationship changes interaction style. They negotiate more than other couples, they share conversational time, and they are less often high-handed, dismissive, or disrespectful than other couples. They choose to spend a lot of time together.

Commitment

These couples are more likely than traditional couples to find each other irreplaceable. They are likely to describe their relationship as "unique." Their interdependence becomes so deep (unlike near-peer dual-career couples) and so utterly customized that the costs of splitting up become prohibitive.

Costs of Peer Marriage

So if the rewards are so great, how come there are near peers? Why would anyone who believed in equality back off? The following problems will be discussed throughout the chapters.

Treason Against Tradition

One of the costs of defining gender and marriage differently is that many people feel that the nature and purpose of marriage and sex roles have been betrayed. Far from enabling a man to stay home with his children or a woman to take her role as equally responsible bread-winner seriously, co-workers and managers and friends will often question the couple's philosophy and deny modifications of work or schedules that could help the couple share family life more easily. Parents of the man may feel he has been emasculated; parents of the woman may feel she is setting herself up for a fall. Validation and support are rare and have to be consciously sought.

Career Costs

Peer couples need jobs that allow them to coparent. Sometimes they wait long enough to get enough clout in their careers to be able to modify their schedules so that they can share parenting. But more often they have to be lucky enough to be in jobs that naturally support child raising (for example, both working at home work stations), or they have to modify their career ambitions in favor of their family aspirations. This means avoiding or changing jobs that require extensive travel, changing venues in quick succession, and jobs that are all consuming (for example, a high-powered litigator in lengthy trials). Many couples have experienced one or both partners' having to forgo career opportunities. Sometimes it is painful to watch others who have dedicated themselves more singlemindedly to careers do financially better or achieve more prestigious positions.

Identity Costs

By downplaying work and emphasizing family, peer couples go against the prevailing standards of male and female role success. Marriages have traditionally defined themselves as a success if the man made money and created a good life-style for the family and the wife created good children and a satisfied husband. Peer couples have to define success differently. Except for "power couples" who can afford the help that allows them to have high-voltage careers and family time, economic success may have to be modified. Neither sex can assess their success according to traditional roles. It is hard to know how to evaluate oneself.

Sexual Dynamism

Peer partners get so close that some complain that an "incest taboo" sets in. They are each other's best friends, and if they aren't careful, that is exactly what they will start acting like in bed. Many find ways to get around this overfamiliarization problem, but the fact is that their absolute integration in each other's lives has to be leavened with some artifice to put romance back into the relationship.

Exclusion of Others

These couples become each other's best friend, and that can make everyone else feel a bit excluded. Kin and close friends stop getting the kind of attention they used to have and may be resentful. Although these couples tend to be child centered and have in fact organized their lives so that they can parent better, they are also dedicated to their adult relationship. This means they have to be careful not to make their own children feel excluded.

Calibrating the Right Mix of Equity and Equality

It is not always clear how to maintain a peer relationship. Sometimes it requires *equality*, with both partners supporting each other in the home and with the children. This prevents the relationship from being divided into low and high prestige worlds, and undermining deep friendship. But other times the best answer is *equity*. Each partner can and should give in different coin, and that is the best way to be loving and collaborative and supportive to the marriage. Figuring out the right thing to do all the time is tiring and inexact. Sometimes couples just want to retreat to doing the "boy thing" and the "girl thing"—not because it works—but because it is much clearer what each person should do to do his or her part for the relationship.

The Balance of Costs and Rewards

In spite of the costs, the peer couples described in this book believe that they have created an extremely rewarding marriage and family. Many of the costs I have outlined are not costs they feel they have suffered—or if they have, they feel those costs are a manageable part of an otherwise terrific arrangement. Many of them have varied and effective coping strategies that they believe solve or minimize these issues in their relationship.

Understanding how peer marriage works and what it accomplishes for husbands and wives makes it clear why some people move past social custom and gender socialization to reach it. The chapters that follow show how peer marriage comes about and what these marriages look like as friendships, as sexual and intimate love affairs, and as economic and parenting partnerships. It will be clear by the end of the book that the peer couples interviewed have established their relationships on common ground, as a common cause. Learning how best to achieve peer marriage and how to enjoy its fruits and negotiate its challenges is the next great challenge in our age of equality.

— Chapter 2 —

Deep Friendship

P eer partners are best friends—best friends in a way that is quite different from traditional couples. In traditional marriage, the road to intimacy begins with a detour. Traditional singles seek an ideal that at best is modeled on their parents' marriage and at worst is a fiction drawn from popular magazines. If men and women are the mysterious "other"—not drawn together by similarities—they fall in love by idealizing the opposite sex. Deflationary information is put off for as long as possible. Hope is more precious than realism. In early love, we feel like our best, most perfect self, blessed by a worthy partner.

When I was growing up, my generation of women was told that selflessness created a loving relationship. Superb female caretaking would produce spousal appreciation, dependence, and commitment. Men were told that if they picked the right woman and financially supported her and their children, they would be happy and that differences between mates—the yin and yang of innumerable centuries—would hold a marriage together.

But while contributions in such different ways worked to make the couple interdependent, perhaps intrigued by one another, they reduced the chance for friendship. Men and women ghettoized their deepest secrets, thwarting disclosure by drawing gender boundaries. Vast regions of spousal privacy prevailed. Of course, marital friendships existed, but rarely according to modern expectations of psychological exploration and exchange. As more demanding standards for intimacy have emerged, these models of marriage and intimacy have failed to satisfy; now achieving friendship has become a critical element for a lasting marriage.

Sadly, many husbands and wives feel that their spouse has never understood their most profound hopes, desires, feelings, and reactions. The intimacy of marriage shrivels each time one partner's expectations of the other's response are dashed. Couples might feel their frustration comes from receiving the wrong advice or being asked irrelevant questions; however, a flash of irritation can mask a deeper schism. Being misunderstood produces an underlying fear of being unknown, of thinking "Doesn't this person really know who I am?" "Will this person never know what I need?"

Countless small missteps reveal distance between partners. A person may feel jarred, for example, when his or her spouse gives a present that is light-years different from anything the former can imagine wanting. The gift itself is not of consequence. Rather, the larger, and serious, issue lies beneath the surface: Why couldn't the giver transcend his or her own self-absorption enough to discern what the spouse wanted or needed? It's scary to think that your husband or wife is locked into erroneous preconceptions, blocked from taking in your true nature and desires. One wife said of her husband of nine years, "It's gotten so I dread Mother's Day. First, I have told him a hundred times, 'Don't send me flowers.' So what do I get, every Mother's Day, without fail? I get cut flowers. And I have to be nice about it. But in a nice way, I tell him, 'Don't do it again.' Want another example? I hate horses, I don't like camping out. I long for a weekend at the Sheraton. What do I get for an anniversary present? Him all happy and tail wagging like a golden retriever, waiting for my great appreciation? A two-week vacation at a dude ranch."

In daily life, slights might get dismissed. The sudden awareness of not being known by one's spouse erupts when personal crisis sharpens our demands and increases our despair if we feel unknown. One husband described his wife's insensitivity: "My father had died. I hadn't been close to him, but I loved him, and I was decompensating, bouncing off the wall—but in my way, which is that I hold it inside, and inside I'm depressed and angry, but outside I just look a little stressed. Annie [his wife] let me alone, which was good since I have trouble expressing my feelings and don't want to be psychoanalyzed. But then she forgot about me completely. [My grieving] was like some little inconvenience, some one-day event had happened and now everything could be okay. She really wasn't aware of how much I was suffering. I got mad and ended up feeling isolated."

A young woman in a new marriage had a different experience but with the same sad recognition: "My best friend had turned on me. I can't describe it as anything less than a betrayal, a divorce, the worst thing I had happen to me. This was someone I thought would be there forever. Jack [her husband] told me he'd always thought she was a bitch and untrustworthy and left it at that, and also made it plain that I was going on a little too long about this. I thought he knew how I felt about friendship, and how insecure I am at heart, and how this just unraveled my whole self-esteem. But he was completely unconscious of how bad I was hurting. I was crying half the time about her and half the time about my marriage."

Marital Failures

The feeling of not having been understood, and therefore without a soulmate, can occur in any marriage, but by today's standards of equality, the rules and values of conventional marriage *encourage* failures at friendship. At least five types of failure can emerge because traditional gender guidelines undermine marital intimacy.

Failure of Empathy

Rapport unifies a marriage. When partners know each other's thoughts, they feel connected. Couples who share a wordless comprehension do not even have to look at each other to know what each partner's reaction to a child's misbehavior will be. Like colleagues who have worked closely for many years, they have accumulated a large storehouse of information about each other's reactions and opinions. Each knows how the other will feel in most situations. Trapped at a dinner party with a particularly annoying or boring person, their eyes meet for a mere instant, acknowledging volumes of joint amuse-ment or distress. Later, at home, their post mortem begins with the assumption that each knows how the other has felt about the evening. Both partners experience the world simultaneously through two pairs of eyes—their own and those of a spouse.

A failure of empathy makes this kind of exchange impossible. What happens when one partner leaves the dinner and says, "God what a boor that man was!" and the other replies, "Are you kidding? I thought he was your kind of guy. I thought you were really enjoying yourself." With that simple exchange, part of the pair's sense of in-timacy vanishes. The shared experience was a fantasy. If there were knowing glances, they telegraphed different messages. Small misper-ceptions begin to add up, leading to worries that the couple has no joint sensibility and is bolstered by the recognition that they are living different lives, with different priorities, that promote different sensi-bilities. Because of such segmentation, they are more likely to have exchanged day-to-day information and feelings with co-workers or friends than with a spouse. Over time, traditional partners may find that they are more likely to have an empathetic relationship with friends outside the relationship. One woman in a marriage of five years said, "What makes it worse is I have a terrific relationship with the guy I work with. If the president sends out one of his dumb-ass memos, we look up, peer over our partition, and we both have the same look on our face. With Frank [her husband] it's like I just can't get inside his head. Sometimes I think he'll think a situation is funny and he'll take it seriously, or I'll be serious and he thinks I'm putting him on. It makes me wonder if we're mismatched."

Common perceptions—or at least the ability to predict when they will be common and when they will not—contribute mightily to the feeling that the spouses enjoy a close marriage. Differences in taste do not discredit the relationship, but it is an altogether different matter to find a spouse's inner thoughts incomprehensible. And since mo-ments of truth occur constantly, from judging the merits of a movie to evaluating a friend's conduct, success at feeling and reacting in syn-chrony constitutes a continuing test of intimacy.

Feeling not known can lead to a sense of being stereotyped, even caricatured. Idealization may flatter, but it does not bring two people closer together. As one wife said, "I cannot see myself the way Larry sees me. He describes me as some sort of a saint, and I'm hardly a saint. You might think I'm being unfair; I mean, who doesn't want their husband to worship them? Right? But that person he thinks is so great isn't me. I want him to see me."

When a spouse feels unknown, the value of the marriage cheapens. We all need to believe that there is a reason our spouse married us rather than someone else. Why would a wife have chosen her husband if, as twenty-nine-year-old husband put it, "she doesn't appreciate my greatest strength, which—now don't laugh—is that I'm a hell of a good-natured guy. Really, I just let most of it blow over my head, don't let it bother me. It's not like I want a gold star every time I'm a good guy, but I really think she doesn't fully appreciate me, and so it feels kinda wasted, you know?"

At its worst, the accumulated feeling is one of isolation, of being alone in the world, forced to face every primal fear without help or solace. And this is no philosophical point: many men and women acknowledge it. Dozens of popular books and movies revolve around husbands and wives who feel desperately lonely even when they are conducting what observers think is a reasonably successful marriage and family life.

Failure of Interest

Part of intimacy, of friendship, is exchanging interests or experiences that enlarge the couple's life together. If events and projects are systematically undisclosed, the couple may not really have a relationship. Two people can coordinate a perfectly nice life together, but merely managing interlocking schedules is not marriage in any transcendent sense of the word.

Why aren't all wives in non-peer relationships furious—or at least sad—when their husbands deny interest or conversational time? Because many traditional women contribute *both* sides of the conversation. They ask him how he's doing—and slip in their own comments when they can, or they provide enough conversation for both of them. Women with a taciturn or conversationally lazy husband learn how to simultaneously entertain themselves and help their husbands express their feelings. This makes men feel as if they are having a conversation, and helps dilute the wives' frustration at the husband's lack of interest in emotional exchange. However, her compensatory acts mean that he never takes responsibility. She becomes the conversational spokesperson in the relationship—and may never have to notice how little effort he is putting into communicating.

Some husbands and wives, however, have tried to share their life away from each other, but they have been rebuffed—perhaps not obviously turned away but effectively turned off. A husband may say, "Tell me what happened with the kids," but if his eyes glaze over halfway through the story or he displays impatience with the amount of narrative detail, he reinforces his wife's alienation and self-editing. A discerning spouse can spot the difference between feigned and genuine interest, especially if the uninterested party has few incentives to disguise his or her ennui.

It may not seem revolutionary to say that spouses should show some interest in each other's life, but it is easy to become lazy and settle for form rather than substance. Simple self-deceptions occur. Checking in about "what happened today" is accepted as fulfilling the requirements of marital communication. One homemaker describes the conversations between her husband and herself upon his return from work: "Oh, yes, he asks about the children. First thing. But it's just to check out the state of the nation, no child development chats or anything like that! He loves the children, but he doesn't seem to need to know much, you know what I mean. An example would be if he asks me how the kids are doing, and I'll say Robbie finished second in the spelling bee, and he'll say 'Great!' and then go on to the next topic."

This phenomenon isn't restricted to wives shut out by husbands who are uninterested in mundane topics. Husbands often complain about wives who have neither the patience nor the goodwill to show interest in their work. A microbiologist resented his wife's disinterest in his research: "Listen, this is not a chauvinist male issue. I love talking about my work. I find it exciting almost all the time, and I come home from the office enthusiastic. But right from the beginning she didn't talk about her work [fund raising] and made it plain she wasn't too interested in mine. Yeah, she asks, but she wants the *Golden Book* version. I may be guilty of too much jargon, but I do try to show why this or that project is particularly gripping. I have always felt that if I never mentioned my work again, except maybe for office gossip, she'd be very happy."

Husbands and wives have abundant opportunity to lead parallel lives. Enclosure in a community or family circle has been greatly attentuated and it is possible, especially in urban centers, to have many friends and associates whom the couple never knows in common. Independence becomes a valued and accustomed way of life, and we develop a relatively protected and private self. Events happen every day and in quick succession. We stop talking to our partner about our day-to-day experiences, telling ourselves we do not want to burden them or that it would take too much time to get them up to the point where the information would make sense or be compelling. But the truth is that we have gotten out of the habit—or maybe never really developed the skill—of sharing our lives in the first place. This is old news, perhaps, in the history of husbands, but it's a surprisingly new emotional picture for wives. As women begin to take on the mantle of breadwinner, they eventually develop breadwinner personalities. One working mother said, "I get home, I'm tired, and I just want to have a nice dinner—at least as far as possible with the kids, you know. I don't want to talk about my day. I've talked about my day all day. Barry [her husband] complains that he doesn't know what I'm doing unless we have company over to dinner because then, of course, I yack my head off telling stories about people and future directions of the company and that sort of thing, and then I feel guilty because I know he should know this before some dinner party guest does, but I still find it hard to report to him, and yet I know the less he knows, the more lonely I feel."

These partners have become so private that they have lost even their motivation to share. The husband, regardless of his wife's love for him, has become an increasingly irrelevant audience. His wife feels badly, and even lonely, about not talking to him, but his utility as a confidant or adviser had diminished, so she cannot find a way to direct her conversation and attention to him. The process of allowing for separate lives starts innocently enough, but ultimately our lack of communication so radically reduces interest in each other that respect, the bedrock of any relationship, suffers.

A husband in a twenty-year marriage said, "I feel we have made a good family, a very good marriage. But I would not say we were exactly 'close friends,' in the buddy sense of the word. I don't talk about business, even though she asks all the time. It's not very satisfying to talk to her about my work. It's not very interesting anyhow. I mean, it is to me because I do it, I'm on top of it. But how interesting is it to talk about sales to someone who has no background in sales?

For example, she's happy to know I'm doing well. She sort of takes that for granted, and she can't really know why one sale is more interesting than another." This husband says the only reason for not talking to his wife about his work stems from her unfamiliarity with his world and his desire not to bore her. But perhaps there is also an erosion of respect. Though she asks about his work, he believes she is incapable of appreciating the subtleties of it. Parallel living creates emotional distance; lack of respect exacerbates it.

As for his wife, her frustration increases as her husband blocks her out. She cannot be closer to him because his vision of her is a self-fulfilling prophecy. Wives commonly complain that husbands telegraph a lack of confidence *in* them by talking *at* them, as this wife, married twenty-three years, said: "He talks and talks, and I daydream sometimes that I could walk out of the room, do the dishes, clean up the kitchen, and he'd never notice I wasn't there—as long as I came in for the punch line." This woman feels that her husband had not left space in the conversation—if conversation it is—for her to react. He simply wishes a safe venue to express himself. Without the opportunity for real engagement, conversation becomes more and more ritualized and then boring. If the wife defensively protests, her utility, even as a nonreactive sounding board, becomes diminished. Eventually he may talk at someone else, and both spouses may feel that the other has failed the marriage. Or she may accept the style of their communication, and yet no improvement may follow. A June 1993 poll by a market research firm asked men and women whom they would choose to spend a year on an island with. Almost all the men listed their wives as first choice, but a bare majority of the women preferred their husbands.[1] The study did not offer explanations, but the gender difference suggests that wives suffer more from failures of communication than do their male partners and often prefer other people for satisfying conversation.

Failure of Respect

Modern marriage promotes the idea that openness builds better marriages, but surely unbridled honesty can pose dangers especially if hierarchy breeds a sense of superiority that surfaces during conflicts. If one partner feels inherently wiser, or more entitled to set the terms or content of debate, or simply feels he generally owns more authority and legitimacy, conversation gets truncated—not only because it is boring when one person is "always right" but also because the wish to communicate is overwhelmed by the instinct for preservation.

When partners have given each other equal status to speak or be right, they are unlikely to be dismissive. But in traditional relationships, with men given both veto power and senior status, they have implicit permission to invoke expertise, authority, or even naked power. Over the years, an unalterable advantage can sow the seeds of contempt—an emotion not so far from the feelings of superiority that traditional marriages grant men, with little or no guilt.

This displays itself in small, but consistent ways: snapping, acting badly, or losing tempers. Traditional wives are not only aware they are patronized; they know they have fed their husband's elevated sense of himself because of a belief in the fragility of the male ego and because his underestimation of their intelligence gives them some tactical advantages. Or as a nonpeer wife said, "My husband doesn't know that I know where the books are kept and what's in them. He tries to pretend we're poorer than we are because he's so tight. But I play with the figures a bit and ring out a few pennies extra for the rest of us." Traditional wives also know that they can't bring their husband face to face with too many of his pretensions or evasions. In fact, quite the opposite is true; traditional wives often describe how they "build up" their husband so that he will be generous and not defensive.

Many traditional wives run a covert marriage, with hidden agendas and information. They may have a private stash of money to pay for things their husbands wouldn't allow; or they maintain secret friendships at the office that they know their spouses wouldn't approve of. When they perform private acts that cannot be openly negotiated, it makes certain kinds of communication and intimacy impossible, and it erodes mutual respect. Collaboration requires shared facts and shared confidence. If one partner feels the other's contempt, even if only in a specific area, the relationship tilts toward caution and, at least more than occasionally, resentment.

Failure of Realism

Idealization limits the possibility of change and growth. Partners should collaborate in self-exploration, but a rigid idealization interferes with this process. Ideally, two people creatively tackling life together—discussing doubts, ambitions, losses, and triumphs—can help each other learn about themselves and forge new identities. If realism isn't allowed, this can't happen. Since ideal roles are static, marriages based on them are more likely to grow stale.

Being constrained by someone else's idealization interferes with receiving understanding and support. Your spouse, otherwise your major source of counsel and nurturance, becomes a fan you cannot bear to disappoint. Dennis, a thirty-year-old husband, married eight years, was caught by just this kind of emotional issue: "She has always looked up to me as the ultimate businessman. It was looking like I was going to be successful when we got married, and she's seen everything that's happened since as well, of course. I have this secret about myself I've been afraid to tell her because I really wouldn't like to spoil her image of me. The thing is that I'm awful with numbers. I think it's an emotional thing, but I have trouble adding, subtracting—you name it, really simple stuff. I can't figure out a 15 percent tip. I even keep a card in my wallet that figures out the tip for you. I keep it behind my credit cards so she won't see me look at it, so I can look like I figure it out automatically. Putting up this front has been wearing on me lately. I want her to know, you know, so there's no secrets between us."

Of course, Dennis's focus on math skills stands for much more; it marks his desire to be "known" by his wife. Yet, traditional husbands more strongly resist removing the veil of idealization because they think their wives need an illusion of infallibility. These husbands play a role of protector, even of father, and they fear that exposure of frailties would dismantle their wives' confidence in them and, in turn, endanger the wives' own sense of security. Ted, a small-business owner married for twelve years complained, 'She can't take it; she doesn't want to know the real score." Al, another husband in a traditional marriage, ranted: "She says she wants to know what's bothering me, but she doesn't really want to hear something serious. She wants to hear something that she can say, "Oh, honey, you're wonderful and everything's going to be all right.' If I tell her how bad things are sometimes, she'd fall apart."

The Final Failure: Dehumanizing the Woman

In traditional marriage, men and women became "as one"—but not just *any* one. According to English common law, the "one" was the husband. Today, women are still encouraged to school themselves in their husband's preferences, perhaps by studying the many articles and advice books on "how to please a man." Eventually many woman complain to their therapists of "not knowing who I am" or of "having lived everyone else's life for them and not having done any of the things I might want to do or be." These women feel angry and emotionally deprived because they never felt that they had the permission to evolve separately and "be my own person." They feel robbed of their own life—and robbed by the person who was supposed to be their closest friend and supporter. When they realize that their children have grown and gone on to their own lives (and their daughters often with guilt-free permission to live their lives on their own terms), they often feel cheated and furious at their husband. One husband, a successful investor, said of his twenty-five year marriage that was breaking up, "I don't understand my wife's intense anger. I'm reading every advice book ever written, I'm going to therapy even though she won't go with me, and so of course I get the facts. She blames me for not having a life. But is it fair? She wanted to stay home with the kids; we traveled all over the world. We've had a great life. And now she tells me she lived it all for me and that I suppressed her . . . and she is now living separately and not even calling the kids regularly. Maybe I took her for granted—maybe it was too much on my terms—but we did what we thought we were supposed to do and now she's blaming me. Is that fair? Shouldn't she take some responsibility?"

Maybe she should. But she and her cohorts are angry at their husbands for "having it all" and allowing them to have a truncated set of possibilities. They see the marriage as a betrayal of the responsibilities of friendship—the responsibility to look out for one's friend's welfare. A forty-year-old homemaker in marital therapy called her husband "selfish. He was looking for himself, and he took advantage of me while his career flourished. I became virtually unemployable. He only helped with the kids on weekends—and then it was minimal. He wants me to forget those years of absences, those years when I was like a single parent. Well, I can't.' "

Peer Marriage as a Cure

All spouses face problems inside the tough demands of long-term marriage. Perhaps empathy is always flawed, and the failures we just looked at, common. But are they inescapable? I do not believe so. We have mistaken common problems for inevitable ones. Principles, not personalities, are the problem. Resetting a marriage according to more equitable and egalitarian principles leads to mutual respect, which in turn makes much less likely failures of empathy, interest, realism, respect, or female depersonalization. Once friendship is in place, a basis exists for all other aspects of fulfillment. But, if we are at all worried about betrayal, lack of interest, or lack of understanding, we fear exposing ourselves. And that is why many marriages fail to establish this essential bond.

Interactional Elements of Deep Friendship

Americans use the word *friend* too casually and too often, cheapening it by overuse, making it hard to retrieve for a loftier meaning. I use the concept of deep friendship to make a distinction between casual friendship and friendship that stands for something demanding, continuing, loyal, and intimate. Deep friendship refers to two people who *both* know each other very well, who keep lines of communication open, and who are fair and reciprocal with one another.

The possibility of achieving a deep friendship with a spouse represents the most exciting goal of marriage. Certainly people marry for utilitarian reasons: for security, for a place in the community, to have children. There is nothing wrong with those motivations and no reason to denigrate a functioning marriage that provides a good home for children and a secure future for its partners. Nonetheless, there is more.

"Making your lover your friend" is a cliché, but the wisdom of it has been underplayed. Loving means transcending narcissism and becoming a friend. Each spouse is capable of subordinating the self. Partners think of each other's needs and come through for one another as much as is humanly possible. During interviews, four guiding principles of interaction emerged.

Principle 1: Understanding with Tolerance and Respect

In a deep friendship both partners try to understand their spouse's preferences. There will, of course, be differences between the partners, and they will not always like what their spouses believe or say, but when the friendship is firm, differences are manageable because mutual respect prevails. Each partner knows the other's sensitivities and commitments, so friendly territory can be delineated from more difficult terrain. Agreeing to disagree and respecting the other person's passions makes conversation possible and reaffirming. Friends can share vulnerabilities, confident that the information will not be used against them later. Fear of exposure by a friend, public or private, destroys intimacy and eventually love. When a deep friendship exists, each friend feels secure and respected even though their flaws are known.

Principle 2: Shared Worlds

Friendship forms most naturally when people are involved in each other's lives. Interest in someone's day cannot be imposed, but it happens as a matter of course when partners care enough about each other's world to insist on shared experiences. You can be sympathetic about someone else's day with a sick child, but once you have done it yourself, you are capable of empathy, as George, a forty-year-old airplane pilot in a peer marriage, discovered: "I was sympathetic about the boys, but I guess you just have to experience these things. When I changed schedules so I could spend more time with Kyle [their disabled son] I got a whole new take on Belle. I realized what it took to bring this kid along, and I don't just mean the hours. I mean the patience, frustration, courage. I mean real courage. I see her differently now. We are more of a team."

Friendships also grow through shared excitement and pleasure. A couple who raised and showed dogs together never tired of talking about their common business and hobby. Couples who do something meaningful and ambitious together are rarely at a loss for conversation.

Principle 3: The Ability to Negotiate Differences

Friends are not supposed to shut each other out, pull rank, get derisive, unilaterally veto a suggestion, or presume a right to have more than their fair share of airtime for an argument. When differences arise, the two parties negotiate, and not always gently. But the style is less important than the commitment to reach a mutually agreeable arrangement in a reasonably civilized fashion. Pat, the co-owner with her husband of a small grocery store, said, "Oh, we go to it. Don't we ever! We just get down and get loud. We hassle *everything*. But our solemn oath is to never give up, never walk out until we are both satisfied. Did I say *both*? That's important. We don't quit until we get it right. That does us good—we always come to some kind of working it out."

A 1986 study that Judith Howard, Philip Blumstein, and I coauthored, "Sex, Power and Influence Tactics in Intimate Relationships," showed that this style of argumentation is far more likely to occur between equals than in hierarchical relationships.[2] Although other researchers, including Deborah Tannen, are justly well received for pointing to gender differences in communication styles, they have failed to show that many of these differences are more attributable to power than to gender.[3] Men in traditional relationships are more likely to pull rank, assert greater authority, bully, or in other ways grab territory in argument; moreover, they argue more than their wives, respond more often by lazily and passively grunting "uh-uh" or "h-m-m," and interrupt partners frequently and successfully. Research on egalitarian relationships shows that these patterns disappear when power is shared.[4] Female patterns—consistently deferring to a male speaker, speaking less, interrupting with supportive questions, and "tag questions" ("That's the truth, don't you agree?") also fade away in favor of more similar conversational styles and privileges.[5] Egalitarian couples negotiate directly, fairly, and without abuse. They share conversation, even to the point of equal time, and the respect they have for one another creates a speaking style that overcomes traditional tendencies toward aggressiveness or timidity.

Principle 4: The Ability to Be Private and Separate

Each friend brings something to the table. Young children might like a friend who is a virtual shadow, a one-person fan club who dresses, thinks and acts like his or her hero, but not for long. This sort of relationship is boring and a responsibility. The acolyte's fear of abandonment can be palpable, and all the creativity and leadership is unidirectional.

Friendship requires a collaborative core, but collaboration requires privacy as well as public sharing. Friends take turns giving advice, thinking of things to do, being the strong or faltering one. There is no pressure (at least among adults) to be exactly alike. Some friends are attracted to each other because of similar tastes, jobs, or sports enthusiasms; others become close through contact, perhaps sharing one area of their lives but not others. They forgive each other some areas of disagreement or strong differences because of proved value in another context. Most friends do not just want "to become as one." Being more than one is far more interesting.

———————

These are the recurrent characteristics of friendship in peer marriages. At first reading, a friendship encompassing all of those traits might seem attainable only by saints or by a luckily well-matched couple. But were that the case, peer marriages would not be worth discussing except as an aberration. The couples I interviewed have been shaped by their marriage as much or more than coming to each other with an egalitarian ideology. One man married sixteen years points out, "I started out pretty traditional. But over the years it made sense to change. We both work, and so we had to help each other with the kids, and pretty soon they start asking for you—so only you will do, so you do some of that. And we worked together at church, and we both went whole hog into the peace program. So that got shared. I don't know; you can't design these things. You play fair, and you do what needs doing, and pretty soon you find the old ways don't work and the new ways do."

Perhaps the best way to prove this is to describe some couples and how they came to be peers, and how this shaped a foundation for a friendship, which supports every other aspect of the relationship. The first couple demonstrates how powerful deep friendship can become;

it can even dominate and threaten to obliterate outside relationships with friends and family.

Mike and Rita did not, individually or collectively, start adult life with a feminist or egalitarian vision of marriage, but a basic similarity of interests, an unsatisfactory first marriage for Mike, and Rita's taste for independence helped create the conditions for friendship and for peer marriage.

Even a cursory look at their living room shows that this couple shares their life. Sports trophies fill every bookshelf, some of them topped by male figures, others crowned by women. In most homes, these might be mostly male memorabilia, but here they represent their shared passion for athletics and, in fact, the basis for their initial attraction and courtship.

Thirteen years ago, Rita, at age twenty-seven, had joined a kayaking club that Mike headed. She was not looking for a man; she was looking for a sports group and camaraderie, and her first feelings about Mike were limited to respect for his expertise and leadership. She had too much else on her mind at the time to concentrate on romance. She had just joined the police force and was worried about doing well enough to win her fellow officers' respect. In the past, physical activity had relieved her anxiety, and so she took on a couple of new sports, among them kayaking, to help her cope. She had never thought of herself as a "man's kind of woman," and she doubted she would ever marry. At five foot nine, her appearance is strong and sturdy. According to her, she tended to make buddies out of men, not lovers.

Mike liked Rita and encouraged her participation in the club. A self-described "gung-ho" high school basketball coach, he liked to practice with Rita because he admired "her gumption." They both plunged wholeheartedly into whatever they took on and enjoyed a buddy relationship until the club's annual party. Mike was thirty at the time, wiry, and fit. He reminisced about how their friendship developed into something more romantic: "The only reason I went to the dance was because I was on the board and felt I had to. No date, because I didn't expect to stay long. But you know, you start drinking and laughing, and you don't want to leave. And they actually had a good band, and so I started looking for someone to dance with. And here's Rita looking terrific, and I'm sort of embarrassed to ask her to dance, but I do it. And I'm watching her dance, and it dawns on me that I'm getting turned on. Blew me away. Here I'm thinking of her as sort of one of the guys, and suddenly it's a whole new ballgame."

They danced until two, getting to know each other with new possibilities in mind. Rita told Mike more about her experiences on the police force, about her close ties to her father and brothers, who also worked in law enforcement, and about her professional ambitions. Mike talked about the end of his seven-year marriage and his anger at being kept from seeing his two sons as much as he wished. They discovered commonalities; both were marathon runners and had even competed in the same races. At the end of the evening they kissed, but neither had a clear idea whether their relationship would revert to platonic friendship or deepen.

Mike and Rita did not see each other until about a week later at the next kayak club meeting. They had talked briefly on the telephone during the interim, but it was still unclear what each person wanted. They did not have a private moment until a break in the meeting. When Mike approached Rita, she seemed cool but suggested that they have coffee after the meeting.

Finally able to talk privately, Rita aired her feelings. Her reaction at the time, she said, was characteristic of the kind of person she feels herself to be. "I am not a put-on type person. I didn't want to pretend that what happened at the party didn't matter to me. For me, that evening with Mike was really special, but I didn't want to make a fool of myself, and I wanted to stay friends if it turned out that I had read his signals wrong." So being a straightforward person, preferring to take it on the chin rather than fool herself or force herself on someone who did not want her, she asked Mike outright how he felt about her and if he wanted a relationship. Mike was simultaneously surprised, relieved, and confused about how to reply. Unaccustomed to such directness and honesty, he found himself somewhat embarrassed and tongue-tied, but he admired initiative, and he was very attracted to Rita.

Nevertheless, he proceeded slowly, because the situation fell so far outside his ideas above love and romance. He had no model to guide him. He had met his former wife in high school; they had dated for two years and then married. Their very traditional courtship had easily evolved into a traditional marriage. "I was the coach and she was the wife who took care of the kids and came to games occasionally. I didn't expect her to really like sports as much as I do, and she didn't. I was doing it the way it was supposed to be done, but I wasn't having any fun. So I got to the this-is-the-way-it-is stage, and I was spending a lot of time with the teams and doing my own thing. And I could have gone on that way forever probably if Sally hadn't announced that she wanted a divorce. I sort of knew it was coming because she wasn't really happy. She wanted us to be together more, but the more she pushed, the more I withdrew. To tell you the truth, I was bored. It was all small talk with her or kid talk, or a lot of gossip about people I really couldn't care less about. So you can imagine how it blew me away to have this different kind of relationship with Rita."

By "different" Mike meant the level of companionship he and Rita offered each other. After their conversation over coffee, they did not date but rather "hung out" together. It amazed his friends. Mike had been known as a "man's man," and suddenly he was spending almost every free moment with Rita. Mike explained how he could make such a change in his life: "Rita is different. For one thing, she takes her job seriously, and I take it seriously because it's tough, important work. If you could have told me that I would rather be running with her than on my own, I would just have laughed at you. There is no bullshit conversation. I'm always interested. She's always straight with me. I don't get the feeling like I did with Sally that she is saying one thing but wanting something else out of me that I'm supposed to guess. I think we've developed a style of communicating together."

As well suited as they felt during this period, plenty of snags developed. The biggest hurdle was integrating Mike's two sons, Dean, age nine, and Christopher, seven, into the new relationship. The boys passionately resisted the idea of their father's romantic involvement with someone other than their mother, and they attempted sabotage, both subtle and overt. Rita wanted a mutually agreed upon plan for changing the situation, but Mike balked. The boys were his problem, and he would deal with them.

Rita unequivocally rejected Mike's definition of the situation: "I told him that if he and I didn't work together like a team on this, it would encourage the boys to deal only through their dad, and that would be the wrong way to set up our marriage. I didn't want to be shut out of anything. I didn't want him to take care of things for me. I wanted to take care of things together. He resisted really hard at first because that wasn't his way, but finally we did talk to the boys together."

As Rita and Mike carved out a partnership, they encountered unanticipated resentment and resistance from their friends and families. No one minded the honeymoon fever, but some began to voice a feeling of rejection as their exclusion continued. Rita's family was especially hurt. The couple was sympathetic—they, too, wanted to see their friends and families more—but they also resisted family pressures. Rita did not want to mimic her parent's more gender-segregated and familial marriage. "After Mass," said Rita of her past, "the whole family would go out to eat and spend the day together. Dad and the guys and I would watch a game on the tube, or we'd just sit around chewing the fat. When I stopped showing up all the time, they were really hurt. I don't think they had ever imagined me married. They realized that a wife isn't going to be around like a single person, but they still make me feel like I'm rejecting them. It's even worse with my friends. Patrick [her partner at work] began to sulk and take potshots. People just don't like it because they can't imagine what our marriage is like. You know, people talk about how important marriage is, but really what they want you to do is bitch about it. I don't complain, because my marriage is different. Mike and I do have something real unique and special. And that's not just romantic bullshit."

Mike also understands his friends' need for him, but he feels that if their own marriages were better, then their demands on him wouldn't be so great. He is more sympathetic than Rita, however, because he remembers his own past, when he was in the kind of marriage that relied on friends and family to prop it up. He doesn't wish to exclude his buddies; he misses them and tries to see them when he can, but he finds himself choosing to share most things with Rita. After twelve years of marriage, Mike remains impressed with the fulfillment it offers him: "You know how you don't miss something until you get it, and then you realize you didn't have it? I could have had another marriage just like my first one because that's what I was expecting, just a little better. So nobody is more surprised than me at what I got. Every now and again she and I will be talking about something or doing something together, and it'll hit me, bam! This is easy, this is great! This isn't boring; this isn't gonna get boring."

It may seem that Rita and Mike have achieved so companionable a marriage because they happened to love the same activities. In fact, Rita's interests include many that Mike would never consider for himself, and others, such as gardening and reading, that were initially minimally attractive to him. Mike's preferences leaned almost exclusively toward team sports and other group activities. He had few interests that would be tagged as being part of a woman's world. But the pleasure he experiences in simply being with Rita makes him very receptive to her interests. He developed a curiosity about gardening, which now engages him intermittently; both also enjoy cooking together from time to time. Mike found he had a flare for imaginative meals, and Saturday nights are often given over to jointly developed concoctions.

Rita made an ever bigger leap: She developed an interest in children, first his, and finally in having one of their own. Getting pregnant was hardly an automatic decision for her; she wanted to protect her career from the intrusion of motherhood and her marriage from the intrusion of a stranger. Moreover, she was uncertain about Mike's talents as a father. He had been more absent than present when his boys were young, and Rita did not want to see their partnership dissolve into a traditional division of household duties, parallel worlds, and resentment over inadequate attention to the children.

After what seemed to Mike like an infinite number of conversations about having children and about their ability to preserve their separate as well as joint lives, Rita felt they were ready to have a child. When their son, William, was born, their relationship did change but not nearly as much as she had feared. Both were committed to finding time alone as well as time as a family. They decided not to have a second child, however, for fear of tipping the equilibrium they had established.

Since they work long hours away from each other, they search for ways to pull back together. Several years ago Rita's boss strongly encouraged her to learn Spanish; Mike volunteered to go to class with her. When Mike had to take an exercise class to rehabilitate an injured leg, Rita signed up for the class too. Mike has a favorite story about Rita's generosity; it concerns her leadership at a moment when his school and team faced a crisis. One of his players was arrested for selling drugs, and the school and the athletic program were in turmoil. Mike and Rita brainstormed about how to calm the parents and still squarely face the issue of drugs and sports. With the principal's blessing, they organized a series of parent-student meetings and lectured about the dangers of drug use and the importance of families and schools working together to help students who used drugs. The program has become an ongoing part of their lives.

Rita describes what it did for them as a couple: "Standing up there on stage together, taking turns speaking, was one of the greatest moments of our marriage. We were both so full of pride for one another we could explode. It is like when your team wins and you know what you did was because you worked together. Mike and I are so strong because we can lean on each other and learn from each other. When I was a kid, I thought I'd marry somebody just like my dad, because I admired him so much and because I thought you should find somebody who can take care of you. But I would never be the person I am today if I had that kind of marriage. And I think Mike is better for it too."

GAIL AND HARRY

Gail and Harry met at work, in the public relations department of a Fortune 500 company, starting out as writers and idea people for a major new product. Gail was somewhat senior to Harry, but they were both considered part of the crop of *Wunderkinder* that were changing the corporation.

In their twenties at the time and both intensely competitive, they kept their distance from one another except for professional collaboration. This was conscious and not easy because both of them are exceptionally attractive and under normal conditions might have been expected to show some romantic curiosity about each other. Gail found it an increasingly difficult discipline: "The first time I saw Harry I thought, 'Oh, my God, what a hunk . . . gorgeous. And this was not at all what I needed because I wasn't about to get into some awful office romance where sooner or later it breaks up and you can't work together, or it goes on a long time and makes everybody in the office uneasy, or a thousand other problems. So I was determined not to show how attracted I was to him because I could only imagine bad news from the whole thing. And besides, he didn't act at all interested in me. So, of course, it's a lot easier to deny yourself something you don't think you can have anyhow."

Harry hardly felt disinterested. He thought she was stunning, smart, and funny, and he fantasized about her. But he also wanted to avoid an office romance. He was relieved when his cousin introduced him to an attractive woman with whom he got very involved and ultimately moved in with her.

Once Harry had a partner, he allowed himself to be friendlier with Gail, and they teamed up on so many projects that ultimately they created their own subdivision in their department. They put together a slick dog-and-pony show and started talking about leaving the company and beginning their own business. Their business and their friendship prospered, and when Harry had problems at home, he would talk to Gail, and Gail, although aware of her continuing attraction to Harry, would try to be a good friend and give him fair and not self-serving advice.

Harry's relationship with his girlfriend eventually ended, and two years later Harry was single again. By this time, Gail was living with someone. Harry was disgusted with her behavior in the relationship: "She was acting beneath herself, like some stupid twit who lets this asshole walk all over her. She wouldn't take that shit from me or a senior partner or anybody else, but she let this guy get away with murder. He'd do all sorts of slimy things—you know, go out on her, or not call and tell her that he was going to be five hours late, or say things to her that cut her down. I was furious at her, and it almost ruined our friendship. But it didn't because there was so much there."

Finally that relationship also ended, and by then it was obvious to both of hem that there was something between them that was missing elsewhere. The catalyzing event was pure Hollywood. After a particularly grueling day at work, they decided to go see something light, and they picked, perhaps not in complete ignorance, *When Harry Met Sally*. They went straight from the movie theater to bed.

Since their friendship was already in place, one might assume that they slipped easily from business partnership to marital partnership, but as soon as they began living together, they started to put their work first and their relationship on hold. They took less time to talk during the day, assuming that they had all night to catch up, but they never did. They didn't even stop work for their wedding; they got married eight weeks after they saw the movie, took a weekend for their honeymoon, and turned their attention back to a joint project. But now Gail didn't like the pace they were working at; she wanted some time to savor their life. Moreover, she noticed changes in Harry that startled her because she had thought he was the last person in the world who would treat her "like a wife." "Since Harry and I were business buddies first, it never crossed my mind that he would expect me to cook or me to pick up me to do those wifely things that he knew I never did before. When I got on his case, he would say, 'Just leave it,' like he didn't expect me to do it, but I'm not sure who he thought was going to get these things done. The tooth fairy? We started having these little grinding shots at each other, and it just had to be nipped at the bud."

Gail hustled Harry and herself over to a counselor to put together a contract she could live with. As she put it, "I didn't want to nag; I didn't want to screw around with the way we relate. I just wanted a fair contract, and I couldn't count on myself to be impartial so it was like going to a judge, getting the sentence, and carrying it out."

They got on well with their therapist, and that, plus general good-will on all sides, helped them pull together a plan for an equitable marriage. They set up lists of chores that rotated, figured out which kind of help they could buy (deep cleaning once a week) and which they couldn't (shared cooking), and set up general expectations for how to value each other's time and effort. They also reconsidered their careers, their personal ambitions, and their new company and how that area of their lives meshed with what they wanted from each other. They loved their work and didn't want to hurt the company by giving it too little time. Their compromise, somewhat reluctantly arrived at, was to hire two more people. The extra salaries reduced their profits significantly but gave them some breathing space. At the time of the interview, they seemed happy with their plan, and Gail felt that even if she and Harry decided to have a child, he would not turn her into a "wife" again.

SOL AND MARGARET

Sol and Margaret had been married for fourteen years when Margaret's sense of injury grew so great that she told Sol that their relationship had to change or she wanted a separation. Sol knew that Margaret was unhappy, but he was surprised that she was unhappy enough to suggest endangering the marriage. They never fought; he felt they were both devoted to and pleased with their two daughters; and he knew that both of them were loyal and committed. When Margaret mentioned separation, he thought she was just trying to get his attention, but after a screaming and sobbing session, he took her complaints to heart: "I'm not to good at, what you call, female intuition—you know, sensing things even if they're not spelled out to you. And there were all these things building inside of Margaret, and she thought she was showing her emotions about them all the time, and I just thought that a marriage gets kind of cooler and more humdrum over time so I didn't take her way of acting as a protest or anything. I just thought, well, you know, that's motherhood, and she's working hard and she doesn't like her job much, and that's the way it is and why try and stop the way things are. But I was wrong about it."

In fact, Margaret felt extremely disappointed. She worked hard as a dental technician for a man she considered a pain in the neck but who paid her so well that she felt she couldn't leave. Her employer made her days continually stressful, and by the time she left the office, she needed a lot of support and affection from her family. But she felt cheated there too. She felt Sol took advantage of her, took her for granted, and didn't make her life a bit easier. She allowed that he was a "good man," but that didn't make her any happier. "It's not that I hated Sol. I've never felt that he was rotten or anything. It's just that I was continually unhappy, kind of, "Is that all there is?" all the time. It was the grayness of it, you know. I'd come home either mad or exhausted. Let me give you a kind of family description: I'd pick the girls up from their after-school program, and they'd be all over me and they'd need something and I would have forgotten something and something would just set me off. And I'd get busy with them—getting their dinner or something—and just real impatient for Sol to get home. And finally he'd get home, usually about a half an hour later than he was supposed to get home, and I'd have this mad on—not a big one, but not quite right, you know? And he would just come to the table and ask the girls these sort of large questions like, "Well, what's new?" and that would get to me too. After dinner the girls would do homework or something, and Sol would start pouring through the *TV Guide* about what's good on. And I would let him do it, or I would do it too, but I would want something more from him: more talk, more participation, more knowledge about what I was going through. Sometimes I'd let him know, sort of unload on him, and we'd have a fight, or he'd just say, "Well, just tell me what to do," or "What do you want me to do?" and it was just too much to handle. I didn't know how to tell him that I needed more of him in just about every way."

Weekends were better. Sol and Margaret had a close group of family and friends whom they saw frequently, and they both enjoyed having people over for food and conversation every weekend. They were movie buffs, and because Sol managed a video rental store, they always had some new release to offer people before anybody had been able to rent it. Sol wasn't transformed on the weekends, but he and the girls pitched in more, and the effect was more communal. These moments kept Margaret happy enough for a long time and kept her from making drastic changes.

She got terribly upset, however, when one of her closest friends remarried. As freshly-in-love people will do, her best friend rhapsodized about her new life. Margaret, in contrast, felt impoverished, especially because she could remember when she felt the same way about Sol, and it hurt her deeply that she couldn't feel even half as romantic as she used to. One day, for no specific reason, she blew up at Sol; she started crying and said she felt she had to leave. Sol, scared that what he thought was a perfectly good marriage was about to blow up in his face, kept at her until he felt he understood her complaints well enough to do something about them.

"What impressed me most, what depressed me most, is that she felt lonely. I mean it really feels bad when you got a wife who is living with you and feels lonely. And as far as I could tell, it wasn't just having enough time together, but it was more how we spent that time and how we shared things like that. So the first thing I promised was to be more on time and not take her time for granted, and I have more or less done that. And then I promised that we would have 'quality time' and that she and I would shoo the girls away for a half an hour when I got home, and I would get some information about things on her mind. That didn't work out so well, so we started having lunch three or four times a week together to talk about things, and we started calling each other more, just to check in. We also started getting up earlier so we could do our exercises at the same time; even though you don't talk a lot during rowing or bicycling, you do some, and it was nice doing it together."

Margaret felt the biggest breakthrough came when she realized she needed more help with everything. Sol found more time for her, and she really appreciated it. "What was really important is that I had to feel he was part of my life, not our life, my life—you know what I mean? So when he started picking up the kids part of the time and really having something to talk to them about—knowing their teachers and things like that—that was satisfying. That made me feel great.

And then I could tell him what he was leaving around the house and what kind of work that created for me, and he started pitching in more. He's not perfect, mind you, now, but I think we are more equal and both using our spare time for each other and this family."

The dynamics between Sol and Margaret changed. Margaret explained, "I would have pooh-poohed this, you know. I would have been the first person to say a leopard doesn't change its spots, but Sol has really changed, and so have I. I'm much more out front, I just lay it out, and then we work on it together. And Sol isn't playing his father anymore. It's like I released him from some movie he thought he had to be in. . . . This whole thing has really given a lot of my girlfriends hope about *their* marriages, because they felt if somebody as unconscious as Sol can turn around, then anything could happen!"

Today Sol and Margaret have a list on the refrigerator with household jobs, including picking up the girls and taking them to extracurricular activities, that they trade back and forth. They have standing dates for lunch and exercise together each week, and they have worked out a way to protect each other's hobbies by sharing the child raising. They have joined a family gym program, and all four of them attend two nights a week. On weekends they go to an investment club together, although Margaret does the research on the companies, and it is generally agreed that it is more her territory than his. When I talked to them last, they were reassessing their jobs to see if there was a way to earn a living that was better for family life and for their marriage. They were talking to loan officers about the possibility of financing a business together distributing videotapes on health care. Margaret says, "It's not just that we're stronger as a couple—we're both stronger as ourselves. And that just brings in so much to the relationship."

———————

Mike and Rita constructed a deep friendship through straightforward communication and by becoming a team that shared interests and gained ways to have pride in one another. Gail and Harry relied on their friendship to help guide them away from their unconscious slide into the traditional roles that were starting to cause friction and resentment. Sol and Margaret regenerated a relationship that had ceased to be satisfying by believing that they were capable of more intimacy and understanding. Margaret wanted intimacy so much that she was willing to put the marriage at risk if that is what it took to make it better. She summoned up the courage to demand what she needed; Sol responded with love and, even more important, the ability to take and utilize criticism, to see his wife's needs rather than responding defensively to justify his behavior. All three couples created a marriage that allowed each partner complete self-expression, that offered possibilities for comradeship and cooperation, and that gave each person the ability to negotiate, in a mutually respectful way, to get basic needs fulfilled. At least one person in each of these couples wanted something intimate and was unwilling to settle for less. In the next section, I suggest the reasons for the deep friendship that develops between peers.

The Peer Path to Friendship

Friendship deepens for peer couples with the creation of a joint life. When partners have enough in common, enough mutually at stake, they become empathetic, they can maintain their differences without worrying about absorption or domination, and they can negotiate rather than fiercely defend their turf. Creating a life together, from two points of view and with equal status to make claims, allows each partner to accept decisions as his or her own.

Sensitivities for past inequity and especially sexism are critical. Specifically, many women come to marriage with past slights and mistreatment from men very much remembered. Husbands do not want to be bullied with the expectation that they will pay for other men's sins; but neither do wives want to suffer even one more additional day of inequitable treatment. This tension is resolved by using the model of platonic friendship—because we all know that figuring out what is fair treatment of a close friend isn't all that hard. Equality emerges in peer marriage because friends try to be fair with one another, not because all peer couples are guided by an egalitarian ideology.

For the first time in history, the labor market and changing societal values have made equality between the sexes possible. As men and women experience life similarly and need to rely on one another, deep friendship is not too much to hope for. When the sexes lived in completely different worlds, deep friendship was lucky and rare. The mystique of male and female difference reigned. But while exotica and erotica may reinforce each other, distance ultimately denies the search for deeper connection. With peer couples, sameness allows for deep friendship; the commonality of experience lets friendship deepen and become profound. Margie, a peer wife of twenty years, noted, "Before we got out act together, we were, I'd say, happy but like on automatic pilot. We hiked and skied and had a great time, but we never—don't laugh—talked about the meaning of life—which I need a lot of, a lot of talk about the present, the future, our spiritual way. When Alec and I started doing a joint game plan—I think it started when we both decided to sell the house and retire early—when we started to work together on that foal [they began raising horses], we started to transcend just being together. We started to get into each other's heads."

Of course,women in previous decades felt they understood their husbands, but the whole system changes when husbands also know wives. In the traditional marriage, it is quite common for a man to say his wife is his best friend and for his wife to acknowledge the role she plays for him, but she is not so well supported and understood as he is. Quite commonly, she finds some intimacy with her husband but uses woman friends to make up for emotional elements missing in the marriage. A wife may be her husband's best friend not because they have a deep friendship but merely because he opens up to her more than he does to anybody else. Still, she feels that their friendship falls far short of what she wants or what he is capable of doing. Faye, a thirty-year-old woman with many close woman friends, talked about the merits of this system: "On the one hand, it's great. I have plenty of time for my close girlfriends, and that's always been important to me, and it continues to be important to me. But on the other hand, it really bothers me when there is something I feel I should be taking to him, but I can only take it to a friend. Because I know only one of my girlfriends will know what it means. For example, for a while I thought I was going to have to stop talking to my sister's husband because he was so difficult and it wore on me, it was such a defeat. And Alan couldn't know what that meant to me because we don't talk about relationships; only my friends know. It made me so sad that I couldn't get what I needed from him on this."

Teamwork encourages quality, and equality nurtures intimacy.

Without equality, subordinates proceed cautiously, carefully, and sometimes dishonestly; senior partners can act spontaneously, for the more powerful person experiences few costs for speaking out.

Teresa, a young wife caught in a much less egalitarian marriage than she envisioned, complained that it warped her relationship with her husband: "He's Old World. I liked that initially because you get politeness, you get birthday dinners, you get formalities observed in a gracious way. He learned that from his parents. Unfortunately, he also learned that a wife defers to her husband, and a good wife defers a lot. We are in a very bad period right now where he blows up at me all the time. He thinks I'm always questioning his authority. I've learned to tippy-toe around his issues. I never just bring something up without considering how to do it so it won't threaten him. But then every now and then I just blow up. I don't want to have to manage my husband all the time. So I just build up a lot of frustration and then, wham! I explode! And we fight, and he storms out or sulks. It makes me so mad that I can't even get angry. If I want to get anything accomplished, I have to be a diplomat."

Today, at least in Western countries, men's claim to authority and control is losing legitimacy, Marital intimacy requires a fairer deal. Friendship is what men and women seek.

A Friendship Manifesto

The standard against which to compare the possibilities for marital friendship is the age-old standard of platonic friendship. Perhaps the most essential aspect is freedom of choice: Friends choose each other repeatedly during the lifetime of a relationship. Nothing but their affection for each other and their acceptance of the nature of their relationship keeps them together. The test of marital friendship is whether spouses would choose one another as friends if their sexual, legal, or household dependencies vanished. The choice means nothing if it is made simply because the alternative is being alone. To qualify as a real friendship spouses would choose each other for the sheer joy of each other's company.

Most marriages do not meet this test. Husbands and wives generally insist that they are friends, but protestations can ring hollow if accompanied by uncivil conduct. That couples accept the doctrine of friendship in marriage does not mean they practice it. Indeed, they cannot practice it when they are living non-overlapping lives with different rights and privileges. To be friends, one has to be able to take the other person's point of view. The best way to do that is to live that person's day-to-day life. There is a different bond between young parents who have shared the 2 A.M. feeding than between the wife who hasn't slept and her well-rested husband who inquires solicitously the next morning about the night.

The Problem of Hierarchy

Conceding the husband's slightly senior status has been the velvet noose for many marriages. It is seductively attractive, since it can efficiently curtail or end arguments, and comfortingly continue traditional values and practices. Even modestly egalitarian marriage can seem like such an improvement over more dictatorial systems that a smidgen of inequality hardly feels like a threat to intimacy and friendship.

Yet it is. Using nonromantic friendship as the standard, it seems clear that any friendship in which one person could always (or even more often) invoke the final word would not be satisfying for very long. Friendship requires that neither partner in the relationship consistently control activities or decision making. While some hierarchical relationships are enormously rewarding (teacher and student, guide and group, psychiatrist and patient), they make little pretense of partnership. They may be warm and they may be intense—or even deep, but they are not deep friendships until they become reciprocal. In fact, because we prize reciprocity so much, when hierarchical relationships become friendly, we push to remove the distinctions between us.

Françoise, a thirty-year-old linguist who had married her professor, worked to reduce the hierarchy between them: "It's funny. The very thing that attracted me was the first thing that had to go. Of course, you know, he was the Great Professor, the person who wrote the Definitive Book. I was entranced. But the mentor-student thing gets to its limits pretty quickly. He knew I was a scholar in my own right, but—and I want to say this right—he couldn't quite see me as a junior professor and accept me as an equal partner at the same time. I wanted status in the relationship. And it looked like it seemed destined to fail because he couldn't give it to me. He didn't know how to make that transition. But he did, which is why we're still here today."

Maybe one of the confusions of modern marriage is that we have tried to meld companionship and hierarchy in the same package. When we all accepted the traditional separations between men and women, our quest for friendship was appropriately limited. But by canonizing companionability while at the same time continuing to grant men (in practice, if not in theory) superior status and power, we put together forces of negative attraction. Told that men should be friends, women feel betrayed when husbands act unilaterally. Husbands who are a good deal more collaborative than their fathers feel beleaguered and wrongly criticized. An interview with a traditional couple highlights this dilemma. Nancy, a homemaker who also did some freelance work for a mail-order house, told me that she and her husband had a "great relationship—up to a point." She would introduce a topic of conversation, and they would discuss it intensely for a while. "Then he would turn away, just like that. It made me feel I had just had an audience with the pope: fulfilling, meaningful, but cut off when my time was over. I would understand with the pope, His Holiness. But when Will dismisses me, it washes out all the good conversation we were having."

Will has no awareness of either his acts or her feelings about them. The right to end a conversation when he feels like it comes so naturally to him that he doesn't realize he has done so unilaterally. When Nancy becomes silent and distant, he is reinforced in his belief that she is moody and inscrutable. His powerful position in the relationship shapes the way he acts. Would he abruptly end a conversation with his boss? Highly unlikely. And if he did, he would certainly know he was doing it.

Modern near-peer marriage is just a step to the left of traditional marriage. It holds out the lure of deep friendship but doesn't deliver. By being friendly and trying to establish grounds for companionship, the husband and wife assume they are on their way to a deeper union. The husband probably does not feel he is asserting his authority. The wife most likely sees any failures of intimacy as particular to their personalities rather than a consequence of inequality. But it is hierarchy that causes one person's vision to predominate and his sensitivities to dull.

At a dinner party, I saw a husband in a dual-career marriage go on and on about his sports schedule. He said he'd had a terrific "three-sport day"—jogging, playing golf, and playing tennis—blithely unaware of how it sounded to me, given that this wife had just had a baby and they had two other children. His wife grimaced at her husband's selfish use of his time, but it was obvious that she saw this as "just Mike," as opposed to something wrong with a situation where he felt free to make unilateral decisions about the use of his time when hers was so compromised by family responsibilities. When he quipped about her weight, chiding her to get thin again as soon as possible, she managed her embarrassment by making rather lame retorts about his obsessive preoccupation with fitness. But she, a top-notch professional herself, didn't seem to see that he was being allowed to become insensitive and less involved in their marriage. When he vociferously insisted that he didn't want to do any of these sports with her, she didn't seem to realize that not only was she losing companionship but that he had become arrogantly powerful in the relationship.

Fewer husbands than wives have had this kind of experience, but when a man's wishes are disregarded, more men than women understand its implications. Women often write off such treatment as marital trouble. Knowing they have already lost the battle for equality, they merely manage the incident. The husband may not even know he was out of line. It is the nature of power that the advantaged is less aware of giving slights than the disadvantaged is aware of receiving them. Men in this situation are more likely to know that their status is being threatened, and they may erupt nastily.

Partners in such marriages attempt to defuse anger over such inequality in two ways. First, they minimize the impact of hierarchy by making it appear situational; the wife is supposed to pick up after everyone because she is home—not because she is less powerful or lower status.

Second, hierarchy is softened by leading parallel lives. The two partners are always off in different or unconnected worlds. He bowls, she plays cards, and they keep their companionship alive through limited family engagement at the dinner table.

Adele, a nurse's aide, now in her second marriage, figures that was how her first, very unsatisfying marriage went on for so long: "Well, we never had to see each other. We never had to confront each other. It was only when I went back to school and started talking to women who were in a different kind of marriage that I tried to get us to do more together, and though that might seem an innocent thing to do, it did us in. The more we got together, the more we got into it. There was nothing we wanted to do that we didn't fight about. We couldn't plan together, we couldn't travel together. . . . I gave up trying to put a life together, and then eventually I gave up on the marriage."

But Can't Unequals Be Best Friends?

Some resolute traditionalists argue that equality upsets the civility of marriage, that being known breeds contempt as well as friendship. They fear that peer relationships lead to a no-holds-barred approach that attacks dignity rather than preserves it. Even less traditional thinkers often feel that even if deep friendship sounds good, it is too much to attempt. Gaps between men and women exist, and trying to bridge them can lead only to disappointment and frustration. Consider the near peers who spend all their time together, passionately involved in the same activities. Although the man is definitely more powerful and privileged, the couple still seems well suited and happy. Doesn't the existence of such couples belie the argument that deep friendship needs an egalitarian base?

Ian and Beryl demonstrate why such marriages do not disprove my thesis. Ian and Beryl are well integrated in the New York literary world. A respected novelist, Ian has written over fifteen books in thirty years since he left graduate school and came to New York. Beryl, who serves as his editor and agent, also is quite well known as an author of children's books.

Beryl used to be even more prolific than Ian, but she cut back on her own writing when she married him. She interrupts her projects, sometimes for long intervals, to further what she considers his true genius. Ian goes to universities to give readings or as writer-in-residence for a term, and since neither of them likes to be separated, she almost always travels with him. They are fun to listen to. They debate and dissect each nuance of Ian's work and have a seemingly insatiable capacity for literary gossip. In a conversation, they tend to ignore the third party, rapidly speaking in a private shorthand to one another. They certainly consider each other their best friend, and it's hard to imagine that most observers would not agree.

But after a long time with them, one comes to a slightly different conclusion. Beryl continually defers to Ian's opinions and almost always ends up capitulating to his argument. Beryl's views interest Ian and he enjoys dueling with her, but he seems to do it as master to protégée. He makes her perform, challenging her with questions that he acts as if he already has the correct answer to. She seems to work for him but not with him.

There is no doubt they love each other deeply, and no one would say this is a bad marriage. But when Ian talks about Beryl, his tone is slightly paternalistic. He extols her work but addresses it separately from the work of other peers. He says she is his best critic, but he looks to others for artistic validation. He quotes many authors but never Beryl.

Ian exacts deference from other people besides Beryl, and artistic couples often contain a "genius" and an acolyte. But whether that is a friendship or an adoring mentor-student relationship is a live question. The gap between Ian and Beryl is not a chasm, and it would be wrong to dismiss its deeper and mutually beneficial aspects. But sometimes it helps to analyze a couple by reversing the genders of the people and assessing the couple's situation on that basis. If Ian were the wife in this arrangement, the couple would seem more unusual. Few men would find the role Beryl plays satisfactory; fewer still would call Ian their closest friend. Most men would not accept this kind of hierarchy in any intimate relationship. They could applaud a talented or famous wife, but they would not elevate her to a different place and treat her as the resident genius, even if she had superior abilities.

People choose equals for friends or create equality in the relationship by staking out different areas of greatness or dominance. There are satisfying aspects to being friendly with either a boss or a subordinate, but being friendly and enjoying deep friendship are two different things. Most people intuit that being unguarded with either a superior or inferior is a high-risk move. The inferior may be jealous, resentful, and incapable of empathizing since he or she does not have the same issues. The superior, by definition, has the power to exact consequences. All of this is enough to inhibit deep friendships unless the two people can find a basis upon which equality can be constructed. This principle holds in romantic friendship as well.

Why Are We Attracted to Hierarchy?

If equality is so rewarding, why do so many men and women embrace hierarchy? At least part of the answer seems to be that we find comfort in the familiar, and what is more familiar than the senior-junior partnership of men and women in marriage? Expectations are clear and evaluations are simpler. It's what we know. Moreover, both partners get something out of it. The leader and the led often are equally thrilled with the situation. When things get tough, the junior person can legitimately say "fix it." That's a lot easier than being equally responsible for solving the problem. Psychoanalysts might say this all flows from a woman's need to have a father as well as a husband in her marriage, but there is an alternative explanation. It may well be that women seek the only model of male-female relations we have had, and that model has promoted female submission and belief in male leadership. Where the paternalistic imagery may have some validity is that there seems to be a desire in all of us to believe in someone who has skills to make the world seem more manageable, solved, and secure. Both men and women are told to look for assurance and guidance from men—for women, their husbands, and for men, heads of state, business, or religion who have distinguished themselves as leaders. (For example, witness the Iacocca or Trump phenomena while they lasted.)

If women rebut this idea of male competence and superior leadership, they can still be seduced by another element of the hierarchical relationship. The less powerful person looks up to the person she follows. She craves ratification from her husband, since he has superior ranking. She performs for him, giving him the power to make her feel good about herself; she believes that his praise or recognition is the evaluation that counts. By being superior, he has the power to elevate her. His compliments, his notice, become the sweetest of all. His acceptance becomes more important than a peer's because he has the power to decide almost everything. Which of her comments are clever? Which tasks have been well done? Without a husband to satisfy, the woman is cast back to her own judgments and assessments. Without one person to please, there is the daunting, perhaps overwhelming, question of where to get ratification from and what it would resemble. No wonder it is so tempting to give the responsibility of evaluation, of one's self, the marriage, even life goals, to an anointed partner.

Being the Leader

The more powerful person gets a lot out of this system too. If he didn't he would demand more mutual responsibility. A husband whose wife puts him on a pedestal and serves as a handmaiden to his life is greatly flattered and supported. Who doesn't appreciate, at least for a while, being looked up to, taken care of, and given leadership? As Patrick, a forty-five-year-old CEO, said, "I love my wife. And one of the reasons I love her is that she makes me feel that I'm the most important person in her life, that I'm indispensable, that I'm a good person. We both agree that I'm the head of the family, and we count on my income to give us the life-style we both want. So she takes care of everything, she takes everything off my back, and that has made all the difference in my success. Don't think I don't know that. So, no, I didn't stay up all night with the kids, and yes, she has had to move many times to follow my opportunities. She is the perfect corporate wife, and I appreciate that. The important question you should ask me is, Are we happy, or maybe, Would we do it this way again? And I'd say yes, and I'm sure she would too."

Terri, his forty-four-year-old wife, backed him up. She wasn't pleased about his intermittent participation in their children's lives, but she acknowledged that they had both been committed to his career and that required, as she put it, "careful care and feeding." She also gave some insight into this bargain: "Patrick needs a lot of praise. I always have to tell him how wonderful he is, how generous he is to the children. He needs it; I give it; it's no big deal; it's true. But he needs it, and if I didn't give it to him, he would go looking for it elsewhere."

One of the rewards of power is being able to compel that kind of service from a partner. Another reward is to be able to command that kind of fear of replacement. The powerful person holds his position, at least in part, because he is either less invested in the relationship or less in love with his wife, or he has less to lose should the relationship end. My previous research in *American Couples* demonstrated that the partner less in love, the partner who could maintain his or her life-style more easily alone, the partner with the most options, was the more powerful in the relationship. This person suffers fewer anxieties about the relationship and controls much of its conditions. There is no obvious incentive for change. Why, then, if both partners think they have a good deal, should a hierarchial marriage ever change?

The High Costs of Hierarchy

The main reason is because wives get lonely and invest in children, friends, or other relationships. Husbands get disinterested, dismissive, and potentially less committed. The relationship gets out of sync. The anger or absences become more common. Usually it is wives who start to see how much their marriage has changed from its early years of intimacy and respect.

Micki, a forty-seven-year-old saleswoman, married to Martin, a senior partner in a large law firm, has seen the intimacy in her marriage wither away. As Martin became more and more successful, he needed Micki, often literally on a moment's notice, to be a good corporate wife. Sometimes this meant having people over to dinner; sometimes it meant traveling with him; sometimes it was that he needed to leave suddenly and disrupt all their plans. Micki, who loved her husband but was extremely unhappy with her marriage, felt that Martin had become incapable of thinking about her: "He is so rarely considerate anymore. When we first fell in love, we talked for hours. Things were so tough, we needed each other's support so much. [They were both married to other people at the time.] As bad as things seemed then, I think we were much better off. It was so close. Sometimes we would just sink to the floor and hold each other and cry. I can't believe I'm getting nostalgic for those times because there were some real heartbreaks during those days. But we were close. Now everything is on Martin's schedule, and if I can't be there on his schedule, he thinks I'm a bad wife. He thinks it's fine that I work, but not when it interferes with his life. And he can still open up—but when *he* needs to open up. When I need him or if it's something on my plate and not his, he's not there, or he's resentful. My worries are trivial; his worries are important. This can be the most insightful caring person in the world—but only when it suits him. Maybe that's not entirely fair, but I think it's close."

Once established, it's hard to change from a senior-junior partnership, even if both partners would like to. The senior person may not know how to get out of his role any more than the junior does. But the partners may be alarmed by the increasing dimunition of friendship and intimacy. One or both spouses may demand a better emotional climate. Assuming there is still goodwill between the spouses, they may be motivated to restructure the terms of the relationship.

Creating Deep Friendship in Marriage

Becoming friends requires changing old habits and beliefs. Men have more resistance to the idea than women, not just because they are giving up power but because they may not have had truly intimate friendships before with *anyone*. Women generally find the model compelling but fear wanting something only to find out they can't get it. In a way, both partners have to relearn friendship for use in a marital context.

Separating the sexes in sports, in school, and in cliques has ultimately done us all a terrible disservice. Traditionally, we did not grow up together, we did not play together, and few of us shared confidences. Novices at cross-sex friendship, we had no models to apply to marriage. While times are changing and more boys and girls befriend one another, too many men and women of adult age have not experienced a best friend of the opposite sex.

Rita and Mike are a good example of people who had no experience with heterosexual deep friendship, but still learned how to do it. They were aided by their mutual interests, but they also had to learn how to share their feelings. Neither had previously exhibited a special gift for empathy, but they instinctively let the rules of friendship guide them.

Same-sex romantic relationships have an extraordinary advantage over heterosexual couples in this regard. The person they are in love with is the same sex as the people the have been friends with. They can transfer the script for buddy relationships into a more permanent relationship. They have no resistance to the idea of romantic friendship; to the contrary, many of their early crushes were private fantasies about friends who were usually unaware of their emotions. Most fortunate for them, it is easy to be empathetic since women understand women's issues and experiences, and men are more intuitive about other men than they are about the opposite sex.

Husbands and wives have to conquer foreign territory. More than one man echoed Freud's sentiments about not understanding women—in general and in specific. Marc, a thirty-four-year-old restaurant worker, said, "Never understood 'em, never will. Ain't that the beauty of it?" That attitude makes friendship less likely, as does the idea that friendship and love are supposed to be separate. Traditional men might support Carl's poetic notion of womanhood: "It's supposed to be different. I have thick hands; she has the slender ones. I'm animal; she's mental. I like it when she goes into the bathroom and performs these women's mysteries. I don't want to know too much, you know. If I want buddies, I'll go get a buddy. If I want a woman, that's something else again." For Carl, two sexes have no repository of similarity, and it is not clear that the differences should be bridged. But the peers with whom I spoke exhibited clear and strong preferences for their deep friendships. With happiness as the bait, learning friendship is worthwhile and possible. We cannot simply apply the standards of same-sex friendship and expect a smooth transposition, but there are several suggestions that can be made. Nature has made two different sexes, but the degree of separation has plasticity. As I see it, there are several requirements for creating deep friendship in marriage.

Reconceptualizing Affection

Sociologist Francesca Cancian has observed that we celebrate love as it has been defined and esteemed by women.[6] Love has been "feminized." In her theory, this means that love and self-revelation are synonymous. Self-revelation comes through mutual verbal demonstrativeness. Men are seen as inadequate lovers by this definition; they are not as demonstrative and thereby are assumed to have less strong feelings. The point Cancian makes, which is worthy of consideration, is that this vision of love may be too narrow.

One discredited way of loving—discredited perhaps because males prefer it—is love as caretaking rather than as personal exposure and emotional vulnerability. Husbands feel that making a living, taking care of onerous jobs like car maintenance or taxes, or just generally being protective demonstrates their love. Their wives see these acts as poor substitutes for conversational intimacy. The men feel unjustly accused of being unloving. They admit they are not verbal and expressive, but they talk about how hard they work for their wives and children, how they move furniture when asked, or visit in-laws when necessary. Are these not acts of love? they ask.

Niels, a thirty-six-year-old employee in a city department of licensing, thinks of himself as a thoughtful and loving husband who doesn't get enough credit: "I do the dirty jobs, the jobs she hates. I clean up after the dog, I change the oil in both our cars, I take out the garbage. I do these things because I knows she hates 'em, but I don't get the right reaction. She still feels, just because I'm the silent Norwegian type, that she isn't getting all she needs from me. But I am a good husband. I am very useful around the house. I am not a chauvinist. I don't think love and chatter are the same thing."

Partners become frustrated when the way they show affection disappoints their spouse. A spouse may appreciate the thoughtful partner's trip to the cleaners yet still be left emotionally unsatisfied. They want love in their own idiom.

The accused inevitably feels defensive. "I am what I am," sputters the offender, his back against the wall, his talent as a lover on the line. It takes a very secure person to respond positively and constructively rather than strike back with retributive recrimination. Many disappointed partners just get depressed and define their marriage as having unfortunate limits. Charles, a forty-six-year-old government employee in a traditional marriage, said, "I guess I'm just hopeless. I don't give her what she wants, 'cause I'm damned if I can figure out what she wants. I ask her, 'What do you want from me?' and she acts like I'm just a hopeless case. So, no, I don't think we're close in that way."

Men like Charles accept their wives' judgment of their emotional incompetence; they stop trying to get credit for their style of loving and withdraw from the intimacy sweepstakes. Their wives berate them all the more, but I think these wives bear some responsibility for their husband's alienation. Latitude in love is as important as any other kind of flexibility, and by not taking pleasure in utilitarian displays of affection, the two partners unnecessarily create emotional limitations for their relationship and reduce the amount of love they can receive from one another.

Peer couples, on the other hand, are more likely to merge male and female styles of communication and affection. This usually requires intuition on the part of women. Our culture overdoses men with information about what women want. Novels, television, advertising, almost every form of mass communication tries to discover women's needs and communicate them to male and female audiences. But who feels sure about modern male emotions and desires? If Cancian is right, men like to "do for" women they love, and they appreciate such acts in return. The average woman finds this disappointing. While she appreciates giving and receiving caretaking, her own needs have been organized around verbal and physical exchanges of affection.

In peer marriages, however, since men and women become more alike over time, they increasingly reach for the same emotional solutions. The harried businesswoman who comes home to find that her husband has had her car serviced feels extraordinarily grateful. She knows the cost of attentive acts and realizes what it takes to keep someone else in mind during a business day. When he takes time from his duties to solve her problems, she knows how much he cares for her. At that moment, soul-searching conversation is less important than the simple time and energy spent on her behalf. His style of affection becomes her own as she immerses herself in a man's world.

Paradoxically, peer men are better at "being women" in the sense of adopting caretaking. The peer men interviewed had become so conversant with the domestic world that they knew enough to perform highly appreciated acts that men traditionally have ignored. Jack, a thirty-four-year-old peer partner, said, "I called up the summer program and made the reservations for the kids. I did the research and decided what was right for Kim, what was good for Timmy. I sent in a deposit. When I told Elizabeth that it was all taken care of, she gave me a big kiss. I'm no dummy; I know how to please my lady!"

Perhaps one reason women in traditional marriages are less responsive to male caretaking (if they get any at all) is that it is often off the mark. Thinking of picking up dinner is one thing—and not a bad one—but remembering that she forgot to get her clothes from the cleaners in time for her trip, and then getting them for her, shows a whole new level of consideration. Women have traditionally done such services for men, but since they so rarely receive such consideration, they forget what a wonderful expression of love caretaking can be. Both the caretaker and the care receiver are improved by peer marriage. Not only that, but the roles alternate from man to woman.

These acts do not take the place of conversation, but peer couples need less total "airtime" because they are not using conversation for reassurance. Put another way, they use their conversation more efficiently because they waste less time with unfulfilling content. For example, Pete, a peer male, was familiar with and interested in traditionally women's topics. When he talked about his child's kindergarten, he enthusiastically gave his opinion on educational classes for five year olds. Unprompted, he conversed knowledgeably about how hard it was to get good backup help and how he had personally cultivated every teenager in the neighborhood. He was involved in his child's life, and his and his wife's shared experiences fueled their shared conversations. The domestic sphere captures the couple's interests as much as any other part of their life—maybe more. Pete likes discussions about schools and babysitters because he participates in these challenges. The payoff for his marriage is that his wife, Davida, feels exceptionally close to him and views their conversations as important and emotionally rewarding.

A recent study by sociologist Barbara Risman found that men who had unexpectedly become single fathers were no different from single mothers; they were equally preoccupied with their children's needs, and their social and emotional skills at home resembled women's.[7] The peer men who take charge of their home life create good conversational partnerships because each spouse is interested in the same content and because each spouse has an investment in the same issues and activities.

Learning love in each other's terms increases the amount of love available. Men, as well as women, are responsible for generating discussion and warmth. Women appreciate men's affectional style and reciprocate in kind. As a result, a hallmark of peer marriage is that peer wives rarely complain about intimacy deficits. The yearning for affection that continually arose in my interviews with traditional wives rarely surfaces in these relationships. Byron wrote, "Man's love of life is a thing apart. T'is woman's whole existence." If this is a true statement of the traditional alignment of love—that men compartmentalize it and women make it their only reason for living—it stands to reason that few wives will feel well loved. If love must fill up every void in our life and our identity, how can we possibly get enough? But peer wives have their own standing in the world, and because they are secure in their own identities, they need less. When they do ask for more affection, their rare requests are more likely to be granted.

Collegiality

The second requirement of deep friendship is collegiality. In its best incarnation, the model for colleagueship is mutual excellence; each good person makes the other person look better and feel stronger. Peers work hard to keep the flow of information between partners rather than from one to the other. Their division of labor is based on ability or desire rather than on authority and tradition.

Buck, age twenty-seven, and Barbara, age twenty-six, work both separately and together. Buck is a booking agent for conventions and meetings; Barbara is a motivational speaker. They have strong independent positions, and they push and shove until they come to agreement. Still, they always talk everything over together. Barbara says, "Our friends think we are disgusting. But we don't feel comfortable about a decision until we've checked in with one another. If I'm reading a newspaper and I see a provocative article, I'm on the phone to Buck, or vice versa. He's the person I want to consult with, and he doesn't do anything without me. It's like we're a mixture of brother and sister, coproducers—you get my drift. I'm more the person to float wild ideas; he's more the planner. We have different areas where each of us has more influence. But we're very collaborative! Maybe excessively so!"

Colleagues treat each other as a resource. Equal standing makes objective and valued opinions possible. Spouses need to know what the other person is talking about, so they listen closely. Peer marriage doesn't require that two partners share everything, but it does require a belief that each partner has some overall wisdom and experience that can be relied on.

Peer partners usually establish collegiality by having some purpose, interest, or activity in common. Sometimes peer couples are not interested in each other's work—work might be just a way to make a living for one or both of them—so they look for a territory that can be shared. Some couples who are highly invested in family life manage to be collegial chiefly by sharing domestic concerns, but this works only if each partner actively participates in home management. For example, Maurie and Clark felt their marriage changed when they built a house together. As Maurie put it, "Our life changed when we decided to sell our city place and move out to the country. We didn't have a dime extra so we lived in this awful 500-square-foot trailer for a year while we were building our house. We did everything together. We designed it, we cleared the land, we even broke bones in the same week! I guess this togetherness can go too far, huh? We were a construction team, and while we had our fights, I think it was that experience that made us what we are today. We have so much of ourselves in this place, or maybe a better way of saying that is we have so much of our marriage. This wouldn't be the same place without each one of us, without each one of us working together. I think we learned to rely on each other then, and we haven't stopped relying on each other. I don't know if you want to recommend everyone build a house together; I'm sure it could break some couples up. But if it didn't, it would surely bring them together."

Another difference in colleagueship is that ideas are fully presented and considered. Both partners presume that either person could be right. Many nonpeer partners mistakenly believe they act as colleagues because they fail to notice that only one partner holds forth, the other person being mostly a foil for this keynote speaker. A relationship hardly qualifies as collegial if only one person's ideas get advanced.

Perhaps one reason that collegiality is uncommon is that it can be dangerous. Collegiality requires honesty. People will say that they want honest feedback, but in actuality they want approval. As an abstract principle, we know that approval is valuable only if it is not automatically given. When a discerning colleague gives us fair and objective praise, we feel great. The possibility of disapproval is what makes approval so sweet. But we really don't want any bad news.

In marriage, opening the door for commentary also opens the door for criticism. Perhaps partner defensiveness erupts so quickly because critical feedback conflicts with the idea of a best friend who always staunchly stands up for you. Sometimes what we really want is absolute approval, even if it may not be warranted. Yet we are caught in a bind: Uncritical praise makes input useless; insufficiently honest feedback may be cause for recrimination if we are deprived of necessary information. Colleagues can't just humor each other if they want to have a constructive partnership.

In traditional marriage, it's not hard to take our partner's side of the matter, since, in most cases we have no independent information about what's going on. Discussion is mostly supportive and noninvasive. But the closer the relationship is to being a peer relationship, the more spouses have to function as independent evaluators. They are integrated into their partner's life, and that gives them strong opinions about issues. They feel entitled to express them. The norms of collegiality require an honest and, if at all possible, helpful answer. Colleagues are problem solvers for one another, not uninvolved bystanders.

A critical bull's-eye can hurt. Ellen, a thirty-seven-year-old peer wife, said, "Sometimes you have to step back from too much of this tell-all mentality. We found that we didn't really have the discipline or skills to give nonhurtful feedback on things that were too close to the bone. So we lay out the ground rules on anything sensitive— 'Here's what I want you to comment on, and here's what I don't want to hear about.' Then you get your honesty, but you can put a line around the things that are going to cause trouble." Collegiality in a marriage, like collegiality in an office, requires knowing when to back off. Peer couples regulate the flow of information just as other couples do, but they include more than they exclude. To preserve colleague-ship and integration of the partners in each other's life, more rather than less has to be shared between them.

Jill, a twenty-five-year-old legal secretary, said, "I edit John's work and I do a lot, but not rewrite it. I give him honest feedback, but I don't crush his spirit—make him feel unsure of himself. . . . We're each other's support system and that's a delicate balance."

The balance between home and work becomes a crucial issue in the construction of collegiality. There is no ideal balance. However, home and family issues need to be given their due. Driven, successful workers often renege on home time and home topics because they let the demands of work carve away at nonwork-related commitments. Men find it hard to reverse their training to be ever-improving bread-winners. Women, whose ticket into the male work world is stamped with the same workaholic prescriptions, also find themselves spending less time on domestic concerns. An unfettered commitment to the world of work doesn't usually allow a peer marriage to flourish. Ultimately, there is no room for a partner-spouse—in truth, no room for anyone or anything else, except insofar as they fit into the spaces left over.

On the other hand, there are more working couples in this book than couples in which only one person is the breadwinner. Obviously differences in power complicate opportunities for collegiality, and there is a difference in power when only one person earns money. But there is also the issue of *differentiation,* as psychologists use the term. Working outside the home helps give an individual a strong sense of self, separate from the identity of the couple. "Cloistered" women, who do not have a rewarding source of independent identity, may be so insecure that they cannot hold their own in the frequent contest of wills that inevitably occur in close relationships. Many homemakers are tough and have strong egos and an indelible sense of self, but many lose faith in themselves, feel that they could not make it on their own, and do not have enough nonfamilial sources of ratification to stand up to their partner. There is nothing about being a home-maker that makes deep friendship impossible, but unless both parties are mature and separately powerful individuals, the structural disad-vantages of being dependent on male income and male sense of entitlement make a senior-junior partnership or near-peer relationship more likely. In the worst case, the wife becomes so junior a partner that she is hardly a partner at all. She is "Mrs. Fred Smith," with no identity of her own. She doesn't feel like a valued friend, and he doesn't treat her as one.

Togetherness

The last key element of deep friendship is togetherness. There was a time when togetherness was an uncomplicated, positive concept. Family counselors recommended togetherness as a way to pry men out of bars, away from their buddies and back to their wives and children. But togetherness got a bad name in the sixties and seventies, when many women saw togetherness as a trap—another way women would be absorbed by their spouse and families. The word is probably still scary to women who fought hard to have first a room and then a world of their own. Men also reacted negatively. To them, together-ness meant too much interaction on women's terms. As one now-peer man said about his first marriage. "She wanted to spend the weekends together, totally together. I found it claustrophobic. I felt like I couldn't go to the toilet without her knocking on the door to ask what I was doing. I actually used to go there to escape from her."

But togetherness occurs naturally when partners need the same kinds of release and recreation. A busy executive who grows flowers may like gardening in part because it is so different from his work. If his partner also needs this kind of peace and physical outlet, she easily gets enthusiastic about his hobby and claims it for her own. On the other hand, if she is consumed by household activities all day, spending more time at home may not be what she wants to do with her weekends.

Carrie, age twenty-nine, a computer saleswoman married to Drew, age thirty-two, a car salesman, felt that similar pressures at work produced similar leisure time needs, and they can't get together often enough. "We are hikers. We're into hang gliding, windsurfing. We have a place on the Columbia River gorge, and we go every chance we get. We both need to get away and get physical. We put Cory [their infant] on Drew's back. We only leave him at home when it's absolutely necessary, and we go on long weekend trips. We both need it so much. I think it's because we both work so intensely with people. We need breathing space. We can be alone together, and we create special time away from the crazy city life we lead."

Many near peers actually seem to shun togetherness. It may be a coping strategy. The further apart men and women are, the less willingly they confront their lack of commonality. In the name of individual freedom or family life—with mother constantly off with the children, for example—the couple can lead parallel lives that mask incompatibilities. Togetherness for dissimilar partners is like putting too much weight on weak beams; they cannot bear it. Therefore, in both traditional and modern marriages, the more nonintersecting their lives are, the more pressure there is to keep their lives separate from one another. Family therapists have written that troubled couples commonly suffer their worst fights and breakups on weekends when there are fewer escapes from the reality of incompatibility.

Peers don't seek fusion; but they seek togetherness more and more over time. In a way, they show similarities with traditional elderly couples for whom age can be the great leveler of gender and companionability can appear effortless. As Jerry said of his twenty-five-year-relationship with Donna, "I don't really like doing things with other people. We just like being together. We do Siskel and Ebert when we're at the movies. We do the Frugal Gourmet when we cook. We are just our own show."

Togetherness makes the two partners even more irreplaceable to each other, stabilizing the relationship. The only danger here, is the more time the couple spends together, the less time they spend with friends and family. If this goes to extremes, outsiders, even kin, stop trying to be close. The couple's isolation inhibits their ability to get good advice about their relationship. A system can be too closed. If most couples have to worry about seeing enough of each other, peer couples need to make sure they are not seeing each other too exclusively.

Obstacles to Deep Friendship

Jobs

Women's lower salaries make it difficult for the couple to reject a husband's opportunities for high income. Home duties get relegated to the less "successful" partner, and the gap between his and her needs and duties begins to erode the partnership. Expectations that family time inevitably needs to be sacrificed help keep spouses on unbalanced footing.

When one partner has many more resources than the other, the road to deep friendship is rockier. It is not impossible to have a peer relationship when only one partner is working or when only one job brings in any real money or prestige, but it requires the advantaged person to be infinitely more self-knowledgeable, gracious, and just. And it is hard to resist outside forces toppling the couple's best intentions.

Even if a couple is lucky enough to be equally advantaged in the world, dangers to their communal mentality persist. Success has its own pitfalls, and the ascendance of one partner's star may move him or her into a new set of peers, making the spouse at home less comfortable and ratifying. Marci, a woman who was having meteoric success with her gourmet foods business, felt herself pulling away from Zick, her salesman husband. She found herself asking the advice of her national and international representatives rather than, as she had always done, conferring with her husband. Marci and Zick talked about the situation and went to a counselor. Their therapist advised them to communicate better, but that advice didn't help. The relationship improved only after Zick quit his job and went to work with Marci, directing her sales plan and sales force; they became interdependent and happy again. Marci shudders to think what would have happened if Zick hadn't changed in a way that kept her respect. "I know this all sounds heartless of me, but I couldn't help the way I was seeing him . . . sort of a nice loser, which was terribly unfair and untrue, and unfortunately for me we still could talk directly to each other and be honest about my bad conduct and what I could do about it. And what I had to do was get back to where I could see the man I knew was there, the man I respected and depended on. I'm not saying this was the only way we could have done it, but this way has worked."

Competition

When lives intertwine, competition is always a possibility. Traditional wives rarely resent their husband's success. Assuming his work had not eclipsed the family altogether, the family's very security lay in supporting him. And husbands do not feel jealous when their wife wins a award for homemaking or volunteer activities. Success in different realms usually disarms jealousy.

The similarity that serves peers so well as friends makes it easier for them to compete. If they lose sight of themselves as a team, one partner's success makes the other person resent "falling behind." The couples I interviewed were usually aware of the problem. Some dealt with it by opting out of professional norms altogether (such as two attorneys who left the white-collar world and opened a lawn maintenance business). A more common strategy avoided head-on clashes by picking out nonintersecting areas of expertise. For example, Dean and Sue both love old cars and met each other through mutual membership in an antique car exchange. When Dean decided to start a newsletter, Sue wanted to do it with him, but they both worried that one or both of them would feel "horned in on." Quite consciously, they divided the duties into editorial and business. This hasn't avoided all collisions, but the partnership works.

Another couple, realtors Margy and Paul, solved their worries about competing with one another by taking on different markets. As Paul says, "A little change can go a long way. We have a hell of a lot in common to share and just enough difference to keep our egos off the firing range." In other words, savvy partners who share so much in common may need to promote difference since sameness comes naturally. These people do not want to feel absorbed by each other.

The Problem of Divided Authority

One of the reasons why hierarchical patterns persist is because they offer a solution to conflicts of interest. Ultimately, the senior partner has the final say—and that's that. Because friends, by our definition, at least, have no senior authority, a determined difference in opinion between partners can produce an impasse—or a major fight. Since friends are constrained by the terms of their agreement to fight fair, negotiate, and maintain mutual respect, there are rules of civility for when tempers flare. Still, people being people, strongly held differences may damage the couple's belief in their mutual interests and empathy. This happens in all kinds of marriage, but there is more likelihood of clashes in peer couples if spouses are divided on an issue, if only because peer couples are less likely to give way to one another. Lenore, a twenty-six-year-old new mother, said that her husband and she "hit a wall" over how long their new baby should be allowed to cry before he was picked up. She was shocked, even though they had agreed to coparent, that he really would assert his right to equal authority over raising their infant. "We fought; I couldn't stand to hear him cry—Bruce thought if I picked him up, I was *teaching* him to cry . . . I was really upset that I just couldn't say 'It's *my* baby!'. . . . This is probably our worst, least solved part of what is otherwise an amazingly harmonious relationship."

Couples also discussed conflicts over moving (for jobs), money, in-laws, and other issues. Although most couples found a way of working through even the worst stalemates, a few admitted that sometimes they felt sharing authority was more trouble than it was worth.

Peer Marriage in a Nonpeer-Marriage World

A couple who likes each other chooses to spend a lot of time together. As the intimacy of the couple supplants old alliances, friends and relatives feel displaced by the intense marital friendship. Rita noted jealousy among her family, her friends, and her partner, and she's not alone. David, a medical researcher, said, "It's not subtle. I get complaints from my golfing group because I've cut back time—from my quartet because it used to be twice a week, from my parents, you name it. But there's only so much time. And I want more time with Marlene, pure and simple."

More subtly, antagonism grows when peer relationships expose the limits of traditional marriage. Conventional couples often excuse themselves from further attempts at best friendship by invoking a belief in the ultimate inability of men and women to bridge the gender gulf. Couples who assure themselves that they have done what is humanly possible feel less disappointed with their relationship's shortcomings. They can even feel happy about their marriage by dropping the standards of platonic friendship and creating a standard especially keyed to the marriage they have. It is better to believe in limited male-female intimacy than to think that deep friendship exists, but not for you.

The presence of a real peer marriage upsets these maneuvers. Onlookers may have to admit that they have deceived themselves about their relationship's potential. Nina, a previously traditional wife, said, "When I saw the way Barbara and Arthur communicated, I knew I wanted nothing less—no matter what it took to get there."

If even one member of the couple reevaluates the marriage, it destabilizes their previous bargain. Rather than delve into the possibilities, a very traditional couple may condemn the peer couple. Peer couples have said that close friends have verbally attacked them, saying such things as, "You are huddling together trying to evade the world" or, to the man, "You're a wimp or henpecked in this relationship." Women have been criticized as "obsessive" or "deserting friends for someone who will sooner or later disappoint you." Support may be given to older couples. Elderly men seem to be released from sex-role requirements. Their new delight in helping around the house or enjoying their wife's company is considered "sweet" or touching. But younger men are seen as deserting male gender norms, and many women told me that friends and family members simply would not believe that the marriage was as satisfying as reported.

It would be preferable if the reaction instead was to be inspired and imitative, but most people hesitate to undo the premises of their lives. And, in general, many people believe that egalitarian marriages are unnatural, unattainable, or not what they seem to be. It is only the peer couples themselves who are mystified at other people's estimation of how hard or how rare their marriage must be.

A Final Thought

Can you have too much deep friendship?

Critics argue that interest is sustained by mystery or, put another way, that peer couples will suffer excruciating boredom. If this theory holds, peer marriages ought to disintegrate eventually or at least bog down from overexposure. But the truth is different. In practice, with mystery comes separation; with separation comes emotional distance; with distance comes unhappiness or detachment.

In contrast, peer marriages are not boring. Boredom springs from a lack of interest in each other and from sharing only mundane responsibilities. If the couple shares experiences or thoughts they really care about, the charge between them remains alive.

Traditional couples have much less choice about what to keep and what to share since they have fewer areas of common interest. Peer marriages can select the best of their many common interests. Having two worthy opinions reduces the possibility of banal conversation. In traditional senior-junior partnerships, the traditional wife looks forward to talking with her husband at the end of the day because she respects his opinion and wants his approval. But traditional husbands are singularly less excited about this meeting. It takes equal respect to sustain a lot of interaction. The reason that peer couples escape boredom more often than not is because these two friends want to talk to one another about the things that mutually affect their lives.

Peer marriage shows how the sexes can be friends. Great friends. But can these friends also be lovers? Or does the taboo against sex between platonic friends invade the peer marriage as well? The next chapter examines how this unprecedented merger of marriage and friendship affects the way couples make love.

— Chapter 3 —

Passion in a Sexual Democracy

Traditional marriage is anything but a sexual democracy. Men and women take different roles in bed, and only marriages on the liberal end of the sex role continuum are entitled to be playful about who does what to whom. Women who have looked for male leadership in marriage tend to want it to continue in their sex life; men who hold the senior position do not generally give up that role when it comes to sex. To the contrary: Men are often more conservative about sexual privileges than any other kind. For many men, it is in sexuality that the relationship of the sexes is most defined. In *American Couples*, Philip Blumstein and I found that the right to initiate sex and the right to refuse it are still firmly anchored as male and female behaviors, respectively.[1] Although men like the novelty of female initiation and encourage it occasionally, they do not want women to initiate a majority of the time. When women asked for sex more than their partner did, the couple reported more conflict about and less satisfaction with their sex life. And this was a reciprocal disappointment. Women did not want to be the major sexual initiator any more than their partner wanted them to be. Women wanted to be "wanted"; men wanted to "want." When women refused sex, men, reluctantly, "understood." When men refused, women were angry. Only egalitarian couples initiated and refused sex equally—and were happiest when no one person predominated in either category.

The imagery for sex between men and women is still, even in the 1990s, the woman who meets Prince Charming and is pursued and saved by him. *Pretty Woman* was a 1989-movie that infuriated feminists; it painted a rosy picture of a beautiful prostitute with a heart of gold, who was also the only "real woman" who could land a jaded, handsome, extremely rich playboy. He pays three thousand dollars for a week with her and then lavishes more money and all his time on her. The fantasy: If you are pretty enough and perform sex well enough, you can earn the attention of a man who will fulfill your most wildly materialistic dreams and make you respectable as well. In the fairy-tale ending, the playboy is so overcome with desire that he is willing to marry the woman—a standard she has just embraced because she has discovered self-esteem, trust, and love. The movie is the perfect fantasy for traditional men and women: The man is able to buy the most beautiful creature in the world, who will love and commit to him; the woman is able to parlay her looks and high spirits into a life of luxury and security.

This is not an isolated movie message; there is a long history of other similar and similarly successful movies. One of the most memorable, *An Officer and a Gentleman* (1982) starred the same actor with almost an identical message. In this version, he is a man on his way up, toying with a factory girl, only to fall in love and rescue her from her bleak future. In a triumphant scene, wearing his dress military uniform whites, he picks her up and carries her out of a gray factory existence into the sunlight of his life.

There is no androgyny in these movies. Even in movies in which the woman is sexually liberated and wild, the romantic parts play off the traditional maleness of the man and the womanliness of the woman. In the occasional role reversal, there is usually a morally corrupt woman seducing a younger or less powerful man or at least a morally upright man, almost universally with unhappy consequences. Women can be sexually voracious and even forceful, but ultimately they are not supposed to direct the romantic or erotic relationship.

These sexual themes are not restricted to movies. They play to a commonly held feeling about male and female sexual relationships that male leadership and control is inherently erotic. This feeling is bolstered by the belief that diminution of hierarchy between men and women erodes the elemental nature of male and female relations. One of the most common harangues about the women's movement is that it makes women into men, removes their sexuality and ultimately makes them erotically unacceptable to men. Alan Bloom, in an article in the *New York Times Magazine* in 1993, equates egalitarianism with chastity and condemns feminism as an attack on natural male and female sexuality that effectively undermines eroticism.[2]

Is traditional sexuality erotically superior to peer sexuality? Do we lose something in the bedroom when we give up all other role differences? Do we lose the mystery of not knowing each other—a mystery that can be powerfully attractive?

At first blush, many people, including peers, would say yes. Indeed, in the interviews I conducted, peer couples struggled with their sex lives more than did traditional couples. Alan Bloom and others would argue that there is nothing to be done about this. If we embrace quality and interchangeability, we give up erotic mystery. I argue, however, that the story does not end here. Consider homosexuals. The gay male world has often been criticized for its "hypersexuality" by the same people who feel that an increase in heterosexual androgyny is a sexual catastrophe. As gay men and lesbians have discovered and often write about, the same mutual respect that makes men buddies for life and women loyal and loving girlfriends has the power to create sexual joy between attracted partners. Similarity, when prized, is exciting.

This is not to say that sexuality between equals is easily and automatically erotic. Traditional sexual tension is indeed anchored in difference. The loss of difference creates an initial sexual disinterest. But the path back to sexual excitement taken by some of the peers with whom I spoke suggests that a new model of eroticism is possible. Examining the possible also reveals plenty of problems with standard sexuality.

Sexual Failures of Traditional Marriage

Failure of Timing

When only one person is in charge of the sexual relationship, sex is likely to happen only on that person's erotic schedule. That means one person gets to ask when the mood and desire is intense; the other has to respond regardless of readiness. This lack of synchronicity is inevitable at least some of the time, but it is a serious problem if sustained. Perhaps one of the reasons men often perceive women as having a lower sex drive is that women are generally responding to the male initiative and their hormones and emotions have to play catch-up. A traditional wife complained about her husband's control of their sexual timetable and how she would like to change it if she could: "My husband always does his personal hygiene before we go to bed. When he comes to bed, the feeling is off, you know? I'd like to grab him before he begins all that and have him when I'm hot, but I don't get to do that. He would find that unfeminine."

Not only women suffer from the male initiation ritual. A husband in an eight-year marriage complained that his wife never took the lead: "I really get tired of always being the one to suggest sex. I feel like she is doing me a favor a lot of the time, which is ridiculous. You know, you kind of lose that magic spark when you feel like you're the only one who wants a fire."

It is hard to trade initiation back and forth when female leadership is only occasionally permissible. Women don't know when the allowable occasion is upon them. One young wife in a near-peer relationship was punished when she guessed wrong: "We were in bed on a lazy Sunday morning, reading the *Times;* we had just had a continental breakfast in bed, and I was feeling amorous, so I turned to touch him and just had barely grazed him with my hand when he just turned on me and said, 'Don't push me. You're just too pushy, when I'm ready, you'll know.' I was so embarrassed. I don't feel like I can suggest sex. I can't read his desires."

This inhibition affects more than sexual frequency; it affects everything, from how someone is touched to what positions are attempted. Egalitarian couples share more positions and experiment more, not because they are more sexually liberal than all traditional couples but because they have a relationship in which both partners have the power to suggest, innovate, and break out of role expectations. One of the great enemies of sexual interest and passion is habituation, and one way that sex becomes boring is if people have only one script to read from and they know their part by heart. Playing the other part is exciting because it is unfamiliar territory. It is play.

Perhaps the most important impact of not sharing leadership among traditional couples is that women can get angry. Over time, the constraints of the response role can become unfair even to quite conventional women. Sometimes women want sex on their own terms. If their lead is seriously resisted, their resentment and anger build. A letter I received from a traditional wife who was angry about never having sex on her terms makes this point very well: "I was steaming for about two years, and he never really knew it. He was so damn wrapped up in his own needs that he wouldn't notice that I would lie there like a stone and that I had stopped going down on him and that I had stopped looking at him when we made love and that I had stopped all those little extras that mean you are making love instead of having sex. I probably hated him for about two years, and he never even knew it. And then I got tired of hating him, and so it went to a kind of resignation and sex was infrequent but okay. I couldn't get him to listen to me, to really see what I needed, but I could make him pay for it in my own way."

Failure of Intimacy

A larger category of sexual loss in traditional relationships is that intimacy is less complete than in egalitarian, peer relationships. David Schnarsh who writes about the boundaries of sexual intimacy in his book, *Constructing the Sexual Crucible*, finds that most couples do not look into each other's eyes during sex, for they cannot bear that kind of intimacy. Scharsh hypothesizes that the couples he works with in a clinical practice do not dare attempt sexual and emotional fusion. They keep part or all of themselves separate from each other because they are not strong enough as individuals to chance deeper intimacy as a couple. Insecurity inhibits sexual and physical communication. Partners cannot say how they feel and what they feel, and therefore their sex lives lack the kinds of information that might increase arousal and pleasure. They cannot express what they want, so they begin to settle for what they have; sex becomes pedestrian.[3]

In Hatfield and Rapson's work on sexual intimacy, the authors argue that "both men and women wished their partners would be braver and tell them EXACTLY what THEY wanted sexually. These same men and women, however, were reluctant to tell THEIR partners what they wanted. They kept hoping their mates would somehow be able to read their minds." Their data come from couples in which husbands and wives indicate a desire to respond to each other if they could only figure out how to do it.[4] But that outcome takes better communication in the whole relationship, more time spent knowing each other, and even more time experiencing each other's lives. Communication in the bedroom starts in other rooms. The more role-segregated a couple is, the more constricted their communication, the more afraid they are to share information or examine each other's psychological needs, and the less likely it is that they have the communication skills necessary for fulfilling lovemaking.

Failure of Sexual Empathy

Some traditional couples communicate well, but they want such different things that pleasing one means the other has to wait or miss out entirely. Quite a few traditional marriages practice "tag team" sex rather than synchronized lovemaking. Indeed, the most well known of sexual authorities, Masters and Johnson, suggested it. They reacted to the cult of simultaneous orgasm, which terrorized couples with its difficulty, by rushing to the other extreme. Masters and Johnson and others proclaimed that the goal of simultaneous orgasm not only made all of lovemaking absurdly focused on the outcome instead of the process but forever had us editing our arousal to keep it cued to our partner's erotic progress.[5]

The critique of simultaneous orgasm was well taken, but the cure had its own side effects. Masters and Johnson pulled us away from each other and pointed out the dangers of being overcome with passion. They noted how people in deepest passion do not always take care of their partner's needs. They told us to attend to each other's needs sequentially. The result, as Schnarsh and other critics have written was that sex was made more orgasmically effective but less interpersonally intimate. Tag-team sex reduced sexual selfishness and ineptitude, but it missed why simultaneous orgasm is so attractive. Couples look for a way to have sex together in the same way, to feel emotionally and physically in sync, to remove distance between each other. What went wrong was to tie this laudable goal to the Holy Grail of simultaneous orgasm. People are psychologically transported at the height of passion, and so achieving orgasm together requires either extraordinary arousal, luck, or uncanny understanding of each other's arousal patterns on a moment-to-moment basis. And yet the goal of intense intimacy was not wrongheaded.

It should not be surprising that there are more couples today who are orgasmic than there are couples who rate their partner as an excellent lover. The literature on marital sex in traditional couples indicates that knowing and tending to each other's needs is more unusual than usual. In general, the studies can be summarized like this: Men want a certain kind of sex; they don't get it. Women would like a certain kind of sex; they don't get it. A 1981 study by Brown and Auerback showed that the married women wanted "love, intimacy, and holding" amid "wine, music and romantic settings," "to be courted, to be spoken to, and to verbally share." While 40 percent of the men wanted a "soft approach," 60 percent wanted to be approached directly, aggressively, and with "abandon." The authors said that the "refrain that kept repeating itself [was] 'I want to feel that I am irresistible.' "[6] There is a failure here to create the kind of intimacy whereby everyone can get what they want.

In the most traditional marriages, men and women have little experience of each other's lives; they respect each other's sexual needs very little and refuse to take turns learning what to do for each other. Eventually, a partner may consciously try to subvert fulfillment of the spouse's desires. I have heard traditional men so angry at their wives' demand for them to "be gentle" that they stop having sex or purposely remain rough. One man said, "I am so sick of being nagged about being more romantic. I think it's all an excuse because she really doesn't like sex. When she starts giving me instructions—less here, more there— who wants that?" At its worst, the anger at deprivation can cause sexual sabotage between partners. One twenty-six-year-old woman in a two-year traditional marriage became furious at her husband because of his dismissal of her sexual desires: "He refuses to make love to me the way I want. The worst example of this is foreplay. I am not just hot by kissing or seeing that he is hard. It's not that I don't want to do it, but my body is not automatic. I need to be touched, and the only way I can have an orgasm is if I get real close before he enters me. But I think he feels that's cheating and that the way I should have sex is without all that touching, and so except for special nights, he just does this minimal amount of touching me and then he enters me. Now he thinks if he just fucks me long enough that for sure I will come. But that's not the way I work, and so I either just fake it to get it over with or enjoy it but don't come. And then he acts like I'm withholding and that this is like a personal way to subvert our sex life."

Failure of Reciprocity

While sex might seem to be the most naturally reciprocal of acts, the fact is that the more unequal the relationship is, the less likely acts are to be mutually given. The most common complaint I heard from young women in traditional relationships was a lack of reciprocity. Older women mentioned it but didn't complain much; they just accepted it. In general, women were expected to give more, even among young couples who, one might think, would display stronger egalitarian sexual norms. But when men are used to being catered to outside the bedroom, they are not likely to make sex an exception. When both partners stated that they liked sex, traditional and near peer women were likely to complain that men were less likely to give mutual massage, less likely to touch them for as long as they touched the men, and less likely to give as much oral sex as they performed on the man. These women were upset that their partner did not have a simple rule of reciprocity.

In relationships in which the women's sexual contribution is unreciprocated, the usual outcome is for those acts to cease and the general frequency and variety of the sexual relationship to diminish. This is equally true if it is the wife who chooses not to reciprocate; however, men react more strongly at perceived inequitable treatment and more often voice strong complaints—or seek other venues for their sexual experience. In a 1993 study by sociologist Janet Lever of streetwalkers and call girls, entitled *Call Girls and Clients: Intimacy Without Responsibility* (Rand, in press), a significant number of the sex workers surveyed reported that some men paid for *giving* oral sex ostensibly because their wives or girlfriends did not accept this kind of sex. In the peer marriages studied in this book and also in egalitarian relationships from the *American Couples 1983* study, it is clear that reciprocity in bed is one of the signature elements of equality in marriage. If it happened, it happened to both partners in reasonably equal amounts.

Failure of Overromanticization

The expectation of traditional gender relations is not only that the man will lead but that somehow this leadership will create wonderfully romantic sexuality that will keep the relationship sexually alive and rewarding. Women want their sex romantic. (Although research indicates that most men are even more romantic about relationships than women are, there still seems to be a great gulf between men and women in long-term marriage). The more traditional the woman is, the more her ideal of love and sex is fulfilled best by gothic romance novel stereotypes: The hypermasculine hero overwhelms a finally submissive maiden, covers her with kisses and manly need, falls in love with her, takes her, and then marries her (not necessarily in that order).

Men in ordinary marriage cannot live up to this fantasy imagery. Although they are more likely to idealize their partners, fall in love more quickly, and break up more slowly, they still seem to fail in the everyday execution of romanticism. Moreover, they are more likely than their wives to want sex just for "sex's sake," not as an emotionally important connection. There are some women who like recreational sex and a few men who want sex only in a romantic context, but the largest number of men and women do not. Women long for romantic sex, and men long to have standards of romanticism that are leavened by the pragmatics of everyday life.

The failures of traditional sexuality stem from the fact that men and women are too distant, too different, and too inequitable to have as good a sex life as they could have. Traditional passion is predicated on the differences between men and women. The imagery of this electric sex is the release of positive and negative charges crackling with energy because of the clash of opposing elements. Lightning and thunder is the imagery, not the more harmonious elements of connection.

Peer Sexuality

The Transmogrification of Passion

Reducing difference can be sexy. Equitable treatment and role innovation can be exciting. The camaraderie of peer marriage ought to have special rewards because of the avoidance of domination, selfishness, and sex role insecurity. It should be sameness that is exciting. Hierarchy and domination are not essential for arousal. The natural ebb and flow of power in a relationship and the gulf between any two human beings that continually needs bridging gives enough natural tension and interest for peer sexuality to include passion—at least some of the time.

The question is, Can we live with "some of the time"? Can we construct a more relaxed sexuality because the partners are secure with one another and find it sufficient? Can women ever get to the point that they find the men in romance novels childish and unattractive rather than seductive and manly? Can men be turned on by the strong, confident, and equal approach of a peer instead of by the power to control a nonpeer?

Both our physical and psychological tastes derive from our cultural experiences. Only some men, perhaps those with strong mothers or with great respect for competence or intelligence, find equality compelling and sexy. Only some women, perhaps those who have a strong investment in being seen as an equal, refuse to be an instrument for male orchestration. In history and custom, sex and hierarchy have gone together. Yet people change their sexual responses over the life cycle. Sexual arousal is a tentative and fragile process despite its biological strength. True, some people seem fixated on a certain kind of hair color or build or shape, but most people have a wider repertoire that changes according to personal association. We change our appetites as we grow older. Just because a man eroticizes submissive women in high school doesn't mean he can't learn to eroticize co-workers later in life. Equality may be less sexually interesting during early formative and insecure periods; it may be particularly exciting after an unequal relationship has soured, or one feels more deserving of a stronger, more similar person to oneself.

We are so afraid of losing passion; Western culture idolizes it. In America and elsewhere, we insist that it not only coexist with but be enhanced by marriage. Self-help sex books for married couples offer passion pointers; even long-term married couples seem to be unable to accept the idea that passion might not be able to be sustained. Although almost every piece of research on the topic shows that passion decreases over the length of a relationship, everyone still hopes to be the exception to that rule.[7] Passion may not be a material need quite like food or water, but it is an almost universal sexual ideal. For those who have tasted it, it has addictive properties. Among young Western men and women, passion has become almost a requirement for emotional attachment. Perhaps no other new standard for marriage

shows how that institution is no longer just an arrangement for repro-
duction, shelter, and kin alliances.

Commingling marital love and passion is no mean feat, for passion
is the celebration of the extraordinary, while domestic love is an
emotion of familiarity. When a marriage is based on friendship, as it is
in peer marriage, how can ecstasy be produced? What happens when
spouses truly know each other and respect each other not just simply
as equals but as equals in the same territory? The theory that heat is
produced by the friction of opposites would lead us to believe that
sameness cannot create sexual intensity. If a woman is strong, will she
be thrilled by being enfolded in male arms? Are these qualities that
excite only when women cleave to a male protectorate and are excited
by a body much stronger and bigger than their own? Or perhaps four
strong arms can be equally exciting.

Ariel and Jake are an extreme but interesting case in this respect.
They both are serious recreational cyclists. And although Jake is far
more committed to the sport that Ariel (especially because Ariel was
eight months pregnant at the time of the interview), both are athletes
who spend a lot of time at the gym and on the road. They are both
amateur weight-lifters, and they find the similarity in their bodies a
definite turn-on. Jake says, "You may call it sexist, but I think extra
weight is a big turn-off. And I think unfit is a turn-off. I like muscle
definition in a man or a woman. I don't mean like some of these
women lifters who overdo it and look like a guy, but like swimmers
and competitors. I don't like soft. I like the fact we both have these
bodies that we have worked on together, and the mirror-image thing
is a great big turn-on!"

This case is interesting in several respects. At first, Ariel and Jake
may seem to have transferred the bodybuilder's narcissistic self-
worship to each other. Peer marriage, in fact, can be viewed harshly as
an exercise in mutual narcissism. But Ariel and Jake did not strike me
as unloving—far from it. They had a companionate marriage in companionate bodies. The partnership that has been preached in the
gospel of marital cooperation is possible now in the most private
realms of the human psyche. Of course, bodies do not have to resemble each other to create a sexually satisfying scenario; many peer
couples could care less about fitness or specific body type. But what
they do reject is oppositional style or appearance.

Frank and Ning are stereotypically dimorphic, but interpersonally, their sexual life proceeds on peer rules. "Some people assume," says Ning, "that because Frank is six feet six inches and I'm five feet one inch and Asian that Frank has this domination complex and that I want to be dominated. That's not true at all. We are both scientists. We are not going to change our relationship simply because we are sexually intimate. My size has nothing to do with my personality, and we are equal in bed just as we are in the lab. This doesn't mean that we don't sometimes have fun with our difference in size. I just mean it doesn't dictate anything about how we relate emotionally and sexually. We were not attracted to each other because we are so different, even though that is what you might think. We were attracted to each other because we are so similar. The size is just kind of fun."

The major erotic pitfall for peer couples is one that afflicts all couples—only worse: Passion is compromised by increasing familiarity and by allowing the sexual relationship to be taken for granted and pushed to the end of the relationship agenda. Peer couples, like other couples, need to understand the fragility of passion and supplement their sex life with the sexiness that comes from mutual respect and pride in one another. This works only if couples paradoxically understand that continuing passion brings high costs because passion is generally produced by tension, conflict, or insecurity.

The Fragility of Passion

The early throes of passionate sexual attraction obliterate almost every other facet of the other person. The pure intensity of desire dominates more subtle assessments. When sexual attraction is overpowering, lust overcomes all. The other person becomes a body, a face, a need, an inchoate mass of fantasies masquerading as a real person. The lover in the clutches of desire is powerless for a time to resist the objectification of the other. The need, the desire is predominant.

When desire has been consummated, the object of that desire becomes a person of a more analytical look. Continuing desire may delay a more balanced assessment of the person, but sooner or later assessment does take place. Newly perceived personal qualities may inspire affection between the lovers; an emotion more like love may arise, along with a desire to know the other and to reduce the psychological distance between the two people. Romantic feelings—tenderness, protectiveness, gentle euphoria, fantasy of a future, and admiration, or even adoration, of the other—will compete with desire.

As the lovers' involvement deepens, they decode the details of one another's personality that were impossible to decipher in the early stages of passion and lust. As each begins to feel accepted by the other and trusts the other's declarations of love, the anxiety that comes with longing for the other's continued interest is reduced. This moment, ironically, marks the beginning of the dilution of passion.

There is a good deal of research to indicate that passion is to some extent maintained by tension and anxiety. Donald Dalton, Arthur Aron, and Ellen Berchheid tested the premise that men and women would eroticize people more whom they met under conditions of stress. In one experiment, an attractive young woman stood at the end of a stationary bridge that crossed a canyon. As men crossed the bridge, she stopped them, asked a few questions, and then gave them a number to call if they had any questions. She repeated the same procedure on another bridge, except this was a swinging bridge and the wind made it somewhat exciting to cross. The researchers predicted that the men who were questioned on the swinging bridge would be far more likely to call for questions—and call for a date. They were correct. The explanation offered was that a heightened heart and pulse rate translated into more general physiological arousal, which translated into more attraction to the good-looking interviewer.[8] A number of studies have replicated this premise.

There are also common accounts of men and women who fell in love in wartime or star-crossed lovers (the Romeo and Juliet syndrome) who did not think they fell in love because of extraneous sources of anxiety and resistance but whose attachment was likely encouraged by the circumstances of their meeting. An article I once read chronicled the love affair between a football star and a flight attendant he met on a plane. She was serving him on a flight when the plane suddenly lost altitude and she fell on his lap. He said he knew then and there she was the one.

Students who meet during the pressures of exams, couples who met while married to someone else, any two people going through evaluations and training together are likely to be high on the natural secretion of hormones that occur when people are under pressure. It's not that these people wouldn't be attracted otherwise, but the production of passion is heavily helped by the fact that their whole body is being stimulated by exterior pressures.

Beyond the initial circumstances, passion needs imbalance and tension to stay at a peak level. Yet love and relationship building yearn to shuck off these miseries as soon as possible. The sexual excitement of the new—the new body, the new mind, the new coupling, the new mutual ratification—is exquisitely rewarding. And even when the initial tension is over and the couples have made a commitment to each other, there is still the newness of integrating their everyday lives and sharing their love affair with the world. Will we like this movie in the same way? Can I please her parents? It takes time before this all becomes mundane rather than intimate and exciting. But mundane it all will be—not necessarily unfulfilling but no longer a test of acceptance and gifts of sharing. The drive for full disclosure and full acceptance creates balance and security. Sexuality remains, but passion in its hungriest and most grateful and euphoric form becomes uncommon. When two people desperately want each other—not just in body but in soul—there is no joy in insecurity. Each person wants the other person to say, "This is safe; this is the future." When that is accomplished, the hormonal system quiets down and robs the body of a handy sexual switch.

This transition may occur before or after marriage, and the extent and decline of passion vary greatly from one couple to another. How much and to whom it varies probably has much to do with the degrees of hierarchy, mutuality, and equality in the relationship. Peers operate under conditions of equity and equality, and because this reduces anger and insecurity, some passion is sacrificed as well. Hierarchy is sexy, but it trades passion for emotional satisfaction and fair treatment.

The Impact of Hierarchy and the Mechanism of Traditional Passion

Almost all great love stories are premised on the existence of a barrier that prevents an immediate and easy match between lovers. It is not satisfying to read a story in which two people meet, fall instantly in love, and live happily ever after. Were this to be the storyline, the reader would have no time to learn about the characters, hope for them, suffer with them, and grow more and more tense fearing that their love will not triumph. Union won or earned is sweetest of all. The 1993 hit movie *Sleepless in Seattle* has the central characters, played by Meg Ryan and Tom Hanks, slowly circling each other for the entire movie. Though destined for one another, they meet only in the last few minutes of the film. The heroine is drawn from the first time she hears the man's voice on the radio, but suffers from doubting her instincts; she almost marries another man, and very nearly doesn't make good on a meeting she has arranged with the son. When Ryan and Hanks finally meet, we know the movie is over. Overcoming doubt and fear and loss provides the romantic hook.

Some love stories throw physical dangers in the couple's way, but the most sophisticated romances do not need to rely on external impediments. Modern stories are more often about failure of will or absence of self-knowledge. Passion rises as the desire for fusion occurs even while the central character is fighting his or her true feelings or as the lovers finally find each other amid a doomed or uncertain future. Passion peaks as the pair valiantly attempts to overcome all that is between them, be it convention, fear of commitment, or another of hundreds of emotional bridges difficult to build and cross. Once those obstacles are conquered, our heart rate and their romance slow down together. Try to imagine a sit-com based on Romeo and Juliet. Their longing would be hard to sustain. Once consummated, it would be hard, week after week, to keep their love at the right temperature. Most likely, their relationship would devolve into a lot of good jokes about their early relationship and then resemble the carp-and-jab style of the modern situation comedy.

So what helps keep passion alive? Creating difficulties that do not break down or disappear. Traditional tales of passion require differences in power and status between hero and heroine—a mix of different male and female roles, of different classes, of social mobility through love and sex. The man is always the Alpha animal. The woman can say yes or no, be strong in her tastes and willingness to give her body or her mind, but she is ultimately responsive rather than aggressive.

In most of these scenarios, the erotic trigger is the physical and psychic difference of sex, lavishly decorated by the culture's gender rules. But it is not just the yin and yang of sex that is elemental; it is the eroticism of the hierarchy that is always present in the stories. The man's power and status over the woman turns them both on. Each wants to grasp what they are not. She is excited by her own efforts to reduce symbolically the distance between herself and a superior force. Even as he conquers her (in his mind), she is conquering him (in hers). By becoming sexually connected, she reduces the degrees of rank between them. Passionate arousal comes to her from two sources: the triumph of this momentary leveling process and her rise in self-esteem as she proves herself worthy of him. He begins with high status and maintains it because he is the dominant player in the relationship. He "takes" her; she doesn't "take" him. He makes love "to" her. She is entitled to say, "I want to make love with you." Women who want a traditional lover have written letters to me saying that they want a man who "knows what he's doing," who "is dominant, and confident and reeks of it," or who "will grab me hard and position me around any way he wants to." Women talk about being "swept away" and "being done to."

The higher-status, more powerful man is turned on by these same images. Just as we can be turned on by our own bodies when we are pleased with them, the person proud of his strength and dominance is turned on by yet another display of it. One traditional man said, "I like to pick her up and do it standing up. I like the idea that I'm holding her in my arms like a little girl, moving her up and down. She's completely under my control. She's in my hands, and it makes me feel aggressive and protective all at once."

Peer Passion

Modern passion, the passion of peers, is not predicated on hierarchy and the reduction of power. It is ignited by its opposite: mutual pride, the Platonic model of finding one's other half. This doesn't mean that sameness includes looking alike or even psychological androgyny, and it doesn't mean that traditional erotic imagery, positions, or role-playing are off-limits. What it does mean is that inequality is not erotic; equality and a mutually congratulatory feeling (perhaps somewhat narcissistic in origin, like Ariel and Jake's) fuels the lovers. Consider the following story from a peer couple, married about five years, as Sally talks about her first meeting and night with Steve: "We met at a convention where we were both representing our companies. We ended up at the same table with a group of mutual friends, and you know how it is when as soon as you sit down, you know—you just know between you—that the rest of the people might as well not be there. He was so cute. Not my type really. I go for—well, I used to go for—light men, blond, blue eyed. Steve was dark and medium sized, but there was this look in his eyes. We looked at each other and we recognized each other. We went for a long walk, and the more we talked, the more we knew we were like each other; we shared some of the same flaws and ambitions and talents. It was like our skins were the only thing that separated us, and there was this heat between us. On the surface, we were talking business and our roles in the company and how we had gotten to where we were today. But that was just confirmatory evidence of what we had found by finding each other. I never do this—I am not an easy lay—but there was no way this evening wasn't going to end in bed."

Peer passion introduces the excitement of mutual acknowledgment; traditional sexuality is more chase and capture. Both forms set the rules for continued interaction. For example, in traditional relationships, women want, expect, and take pleasure in small gifts of love. Some women find extravagant gifts thrilling because they are displays of intensity, intent and proof of providership. A single flower may be a gift of sentiment; twenty-four roses is a display of hierarchy and erotic control.

Of course, gift giving and the pleasure of both giving and receiving are not confined to traditional relationships, but the ability to be reciprocal is. Women do not typically send men flowers. Imagine the difference in a large and open office if a woman or a man receives a big bouquet. One inspires teasing or compliments about the relationship; the other inspires teasing about the proper roles of the relationship.

In traditional passionate relationships, men and women invest deeply in gender stereotypes. Men's strength, forcefulness, and success are displayed, appreciated, and erotic. Women are required to demonstrate tenderness and warmth to be erotically acceptable. They can also be irreverent or spunky or seductive, but their erotic role is ultimately to be accessible, deeply responsive, and emotionally reachable and guidable.

The fact that the conscious role playing of sadomasochism remains sexually arresting for groups of men and women, both heterosexual and homosexual, shows that the raw dynamics of hierarchy have sexual power. People who play at S&M understand the rich antitheses embedded in the role playing. The dominant person (or "top"), having signed up for this role, is also trapped by its responsibilities. The "bottom" is actually the gatekeeper, drawing the other person out, defining the limits of the scenario, and so, while formally powerless, in some ways this person is also the director of the play. By keeping worlds and roles very separate, the electricity is recharged in each new encounter. The erotic charge comes not from a question of who is in ultimate control but rather from the tension produced by the hierarchical relationship. Staged S&M is particularly interesting in that unlike ordinary sex, these fantasy plays and needs may have nothing to do with the real status and power of the players. In fact, the lure of S&M is that often the participants have their sexual world so separate from their real identities that it is the release from those identities that is so provocative to them. We might need a psychiatric diagnosis to know why a CEO of a company is sexually aroused by acting as a slave for the night, but the fact is, it will have nothing to do with how he administers his company the next day.

In traditional relationships, most people could not imagine a serious engagement in such severe role reversal. Most men could not bear giving up the masculine role, much less taking on an exaggerated submissive one: traditional women could not imagine that dominating a man would be sexy. Peer couples, if it appealed to them, might be able to do it. Gay men, unthreatened by actual sex differences, are most likely to experiment with the erotic potential in submission or domination. When heterosexual couples (both traditional and peer) play these games, the real master-slave status is always a counterpoint. If the male takes the power role, the need for exaggerated dominance can become grotesque. One area in which peers are far freer to celebrate difference lies in the exchange of resources normally assigned by sex. If we concede that the poor will always find the rich exotic and the young and old have much to trade one another, we don't need to concede that these exchanges must necessarily all line up according to gender roles. In all relationships, individuals will be differentially advantaged, but in peer marriages, all the material or status advantages need not be male; all the expressive and physical contributions to the marriage need not be female. In traditional marriage, eroticism is formulaic; only certain hierarchical constructions are sexy. In peer marriage, where overall equality is most highly valued, women can wield power, privilege, age, or other criteria certified by a society—

and bring this to bear on their erotic as well as material contribution to their partner.

Given the almost universal tradition of hierarchical mating patterns, the eroticization of a peer is a revolutionary aspiration and accomplishment. But recent social change has begun to favor eroticization of a similar other. Women are now able to achieve status, power, and independence themselves that formerly could be attained only by attachment to a man, and so the desire to eroticize difference may be withering away. Women can now derive respect in a man's world, and so some men find themselves admiring and falling in love with fellow workers. The heroine in a film like *Working Girl* may be partly the traditional rags-to-riches, socially mobile secretary, but she is also the woman who by sheer guts pulls herself to an executive position and is desirable not only because she is a sexy woman but also because she and her executive lover are adrenalized by their ability to pull off a big business coup together. One thirty-one-year-old woman in a peer couple talked about the evolution of her erotic imagery: "I used to be a real market for women's books. I wanted men who fit the stereotype of Clark Gable or Kevin Costner—you know, few words, and when they are delivered they are real zingers, and there is a lot of eye contact and passion, and that's about as much talking as you get. Maybe it was dating all these guys who were really like that, but even as fantasy objects, I got tired of those guys. I got tired of men who didn't want to explore a feeling or who were only loving when they had a hard-on. I fell in love the first time sharing *Prince of Tides* with the guy I was dating, and I fell in love with Eric [her husband] over a discussion of *Eyes on the Prize*. The sexy thing was the conversation and the quality of our minds and the sensibility of our discussion. I can't imagine anything more boring—and ultimately unsexy—than a man—and I don't care if he looked like Robert Redford and earned like Donald Trump—who had nothing to say or if he did didn't get turned on by what I was saying."

A similar dynamic has operated to allow men to eroticize women who are like themselves. To be drawn to a powerful woman means to eroticize male traits, which once was considered almost homosexual and therefore taboo. Narcissism as the admiration of the self or the self in others had to be reinterpreted as acceptable and not emasculating, and this has taken a slow evolution, first experienced only by men most confident of their masculinity and least worried about the stability of their sexuality. One has to like oneself and be secure to be attracted to someone who is clearly an extension of recognized personal characteristics. A man who is attracted to a woman who is a rugged individualist either has to recognize and approve of that characteristic in himself or know that he is not such a person yet feel secure in what he is so as to admire this "male" quality in another without feeling less male himself. That requires emotional security and self-confidence.

It is not certain how equality becomes an erotic trigger, but most such peer stories begin with admiration. A typical story generally includes physical attraction coupled with mental attraction and a strong sense of "matchedness" and "comfort." Even couples who were fixed up or started seeing each other on a blind date generally recounted some form of seeming "right for each other" from early on. This was not true for couples who did not start out as peers. Traditional couples who evolved into peer couples found their conflict over equal rights terribly upsetting in the beginning, but ultimately it became erotically interesting.

Marie and Tim spent the first fifteen years of their marriage in a traditional arrangement; Marie took care of the children, and Tim was the breadwinner. But after Marie's last child entered kindergarten, she gave voice to the parts of her life that were increasingly upsetting to her: she was always responsible for picking things up, and she never got to organize her day the way she wanted. She went back to work, first part time and then full time, and she went to night school to get some language training. She met a man there and had a brief affair, which appalled her; extramarital sex was completely against every value, especially religious value, she held (including the values of equality and equity). She tearfully confessed to Tim what had happened and asked him to go into counseling with her. After a period of rage and distress, he agreed, and they began reworking their relationship according to each person's feelings of what was fair and what kind of life each felt entitled to within the framework of fairness. They hoped their relationship would get better. What surprised them was that their sex life improved. Tim found it "amazing how you think you know someone, and then they do something unthinkable, and then you have to look at them completely differently. And I realized that I wasn't seeing Marie very clearly—not seeing anything that wasn't convenient to see. So during this period of stress, I started to see her sexually differently too. I saw her as an individual again, and I saw her as more sexy and—this is odd—more womanly. I didn't see me as just turning over and us being tender, but you know, kind of doing this by rote—but rather someone I had to take account of, someone with an independent sexuality. I admit, it's taken a long time to forgive her for betraying me and the family like she did, but I guess if there is a silver lining in this cloud, one of them would have to be that our sex life is more intimate and more aware of each other in a good way."

Marie agreed: "One of the unexpected changes has been the way we make love, the way we approach sex. Before, I think it was pretty conventional. I believe Tim was attracted to me, but I also think he was unaware of me as a unique sexual being with unique sexual emotions and needs. I almost think he made love to me like a generic woman. Nobody takes anything for granted anymore, and I feel like our attraction is between two people and not between a husband and his wife. I wouldn't prescribe the hell we have been through as part of a new sex therapy, but I definitely think we have become sexually different as well as different in other ways."

Reinventing Sexual Acts

When equality has become the mode of entry into a relationship or it has become established, over time, as a marital goal, some peer marriages have a new problem: dealing with the hierarchical connotations of sexual acts. Andrea Dworkin's *Intercourse* argues that by its very nature intercourse is hierarchical and therefore has no place in an egalitarian relationship.[9] This is, of course, a polemic—intercourse is not at risk of disappearing from heterosexual sexual relationships— but the author's provocative thesis is that acts have a universal and eternal meaning that cannot be modified under new interpretations. The peer theory, by contrast, takes the position that acts are imbued with meaning from the social circumstances of people's lives. Hierarchy is not the only imagery that must be evoked by penetration. It is possible to interpret penetration as the man's being welcomed by the woman, or as the penis and vagina interlocking in the ultimate transformation of two bodies into one. When equality exists, the symbolism of many acts can be transformed into egalitarian exchanges.

Penetration need not imply control, not even to the most ardent feminist. For a comparison, consider the male homosexual relationship in which who is "on top" has nothing to do with who has the greater power or status in the relationship.[10] The man who is penetrated may be the orchestrator of the sexual scenario and may be the more powerful member of the couple.

In fact, gay men and lesbians are masters at changing the meaning of common acts. They would thoroughly disagree with the Greek-American man who contemptuously said to me, "There are three kinds of men in Greece: men who screw men, men who screw men and women, and homosexuals." (To him, the homosexuals were the men who were on the bottom, who were "screwed.") Male partners frequently trade off who will penetrate and who will be penetrated. Even this division of sexual position is not necessary to sustain an egalitarian relationship. Position in a peer gay relationship is merely a personal taste and not a display of a more general hierarchy. If there is imagery of domination and submission expressed during passion, it is part of the play of sexual exaltation and not a reflection of who will later do the dishes and take out the trash. This is the kind of transformation peer heterosexual couples can accomplish as well. The couple is freed to be more passionate because they are less undermined by previous associations of specific acts.

Nancie and Pete are both lawyers who are impressively combative in their respective roles as criminal defense attorney and family law practitioner. When asked about sex and political correctness in sex, Nancie laughed: "I think any couple that has to worry about politics in bed had better go see a therapist! I remember when I was dating really insensitive, dishonest bastards. I don't care if I was on top of them; I knew their head was on wrong and whatever I was doing, they wouldn't really respect me. Pete and I have such a great partnership that there is a great comfort we have together in bed. I don't think he has performance anxieties, and neither do I. We do a lot of 'isn't this nice sex,' and occasionally we do something moderately kinky, like take turns tying each other to the bed! I think the pressure is off because things aren't symbolic of other issues. We're way past that."

Another woman in a peer marriage, Greta, a thirty-two-year-old bookkeeper, mentioned how oral sex was different in an egalitarian relationship: "We don't have to do a counting of who does what how many times. I used to do that because I felt if I didn't, I wouldn't get my fair share. The guy would do just what it took to get you excited or get you excited enough to do what he was waiting for for himself— when things are out of balance between you emotionally, nothing really feels really reciprocal in bed. Once you are in a relationship with real give and take then you relax and you give and give and they give and give—and it's real nice."

As provocative as Andrea Dworkin's discussion of penetration is, oral sex is perhaps a better source of insights into the hierarchy of sexual acts. What is the power imagery of cunnilingus or fellatio? Is a man who performs oral sex to his wife a supplicant, slavishly bending to the sexual will of the woman looking down on him? Or is he showing his control over her? Is her passion meaningful to him primarily because he is invoking it? Is that sex a fulfillment of her sexual fantasy or his? The act is malleable to the meaning. The myriad of meanings available can make or break the potential for magic during lovemaking.

Fellatio presents the same ambiguities, and the meaning can change in an instant. If the man lies back passively, is he giving himself up to her control, or does he see her as doing his bidding? Is a freely given act changed if the person asks for it to continue longer than the person intended to give it? Many women, for example, have enjoyed fellatio right up to the moment when they picked their head up, only to have it pushed down, sometimes aggressively.

Maryann, a wife in a more or less conventional marriage of five years, says that fellatio has been a problem from the start of their relationship: "I enjoyed it at first. I hadn't had any experience with it, and I was curious. But it has become a chore. He takes a long time to come, and my jaw is always aching, which makes the whole thing more like work than anything else. It's real important to him, so I do it, but it's not something I really enjoy. I think the alienating part of this is that I don't think he notices that I'm not comfortable. Or maybe he does, and he doesn't care enough to do something about it."

A more egalitarian couple, Jeff, age forty-eight and Antonia, age forty-five, provided a sharp contrast when they talked about their first experience with oral sex together. Jeff said, "I had kind of specific feelings about how I wanted her to go down on me. And Antonia is kind of touchy if she feels her dignity is being attacked or anything, so I just proceeded slowly, like showed her a model approach by the way I went down on her and she used that model to go down on me. I would start and ask her if she liked this or this and was this right or not—you know, harder, softer, etc. Then she did the same thing for me. I figure I need to learn and she needs to learn and why pretend we know anything just by doing it? I don't see why everyone wouldn't want to know exactly what to do, so you ask."

When Jeff met Antonia, he had been single for three years and was beginning to hate it. He met her at a local precinct meeting, and although he noticed her physically, she drew his attention by her articulate and impassioned political activism. They were both concerned about a local zoning issue, and he invited her out for coffee to talk about it. There was more than casual interest right away, and after dating a few times, he found himself in her apartment getting ready to have sex together after her teenage daughter had gone out on a date. Jeff said, "I was a little nervous because even though Katrina had gone out, I was still in this family situation, and I wasn't sure what the right thing to do was. But the great thing was that Antonia realized I was nervous, and we got to talk about it, and it was comfortable, friendly, open—really made me kind of fill up with respect and emotion for her. And when we made love, it stayed that way. We laughed and we played and it was heady, and I felt in love right then. I didn't trust it, of course, but it never changed from that. The sex and the friendship were intertwined from the beginning. I don't want to use this word because it makes it sound unexciting and it wasn't. As a compliment I want to say it was comfortable and it stayed comfortable."

The Problems of Peer Passion

It would be misleading to say all peer sex is comfortable and satisfactory while traditional sex is necessarily either passionate or disappointing, and certainly not all women in traditional sexual relationships are angry or deprived. The leadership role of the male in traditional marriage is exactly what some women want, and many traditional men are thoughtful and skillful lovers who do not insist on control in bed or insensitively follow only their own desires, though they have the power to do so.

Peer couples have their flaws too. The most common among them is that sex can get *too* comfortable. Consider Rebecca and David, a couple who met after Rebecca had been "around" quite a bit whereas David was more sexually conventional. They met through a personals ad in *New York Magazine*. The first time David saw Rebecca, he experienced a pure adrenaline rush: "I was sitting at this restaurant, and this really fantastic-looking, long-legged, long-dark-haired woman comes through the door, and I think, why can't this be the one who is coming to have lunch with me? When right then she mentions my name to the maitre d' and he leads her to my table. I was so shocked, and my heart was pumping. Well, you know, I had all the classic signs. I even lost my appetite. We went out the next night, and afterward we went back to her place and barely made it through the door before we had our clothes off. That night was great, just great. Sometimes now I think about that night and miss the intensity. I don't mean to say we don't have a good time now, but it's not exactly the same."

David had dated only three women before he met his first wife. Although his marital sex life had declined as the marriage began to fail, the relationship had been satisfactory in the beginning. It was traditional—he initiated, she accepted—but "when we were getting along well, it was great. I felt tender, and I wanted to make her feel great, and when I would, I would feel great." David's first wife had ceded sexual control to her husband, and they both found that arrangement erotic and exciting. He felt forceful, masculine, and potent. The first night with Rebecca astonished him because she was an equal partner in lust and initiation. Partly intimidated and totally fascinated, he loved her earthiness and enjoyed sex with her intensely.

Rebecca found David's sexual assumptions a little offputting: "When you first go to bed with somebody, you're not conscious of technique. If you want them, like I wanted David, you're just delighted to be in his arms. The first time we had sex together, I knew he was somebody very special, and I didn't care about exactly how we made love. But in the back of my mind, even though I was enjoying it, I was watching him place my body this way and that way and kind of anticipate what I wanted instead of waiting to see how I reacted— and a little part of me was thinking, 'Uh, oh. Maybe this guy is more traditional than I thought.' And just that little bit of thought made me not a 100 percent into it."

Rebecca was self-confident, experienced, and adventurous in bed. David was loving, attentive, and more orderly in his approach to sex. Rebecca loved David's solicitude, especially because the main love affair in her life had been with a charismatic campus activist who had treated her badly, eroded her self-esteem, and made her promise herself that she would never let someone walk all over her like that again. She knew David was the kind of man she wanted, but she knew their sex life was not as passionate as it had been in some of her less emotionally fulfilling relationships. She worried that her past love affairs had made her a "passion junkie." She analyzed what the differences were with David and what she could do to make sex better. "I was a lot more active than anybody he'd slept with. I wouldn't wait for him to start things. I'd made sure that everything he did to me I would do to him. And I'd like to seize control for a little while and show him that it was fun to let someone make love to him, instead of him always having to do all the work. He never resented anything I did, but sometimes I think he was either intimidated or confused about what I expected from him. I think he felt, at least in the beginning, a little inadequate. The good thing was that we could talk about it, and once he got used to me, it was just a matter of time until things got better."

David recalls that period in their sex life as both wonderful and horrible: "In the beginning, I couldn't get it up all the time because I was so full of emotion and anxiety over pleasing her that I was overexcited. I was really dismayed that my body wouldn't cooperate. I was trying to pretend it wasn't happening, but Becky was real open about the issue. Once I learned we could just let things happen between us, and I didn't have to be in charge to give us both a good time, I relaxed enormously. I've never had the problem since that time, which isn't to say our sex life is perfect. We still have our problems, but I think the give and take in bed between us works very well."

The main problem they do have is that they don't make love often. They have different explanations for the lack of frequency. David blames work, the demands of child raising, life in general. Rebecca thinks that that is all true, but she is more worried that something is more fundamentally problematic about their relationship: "David is more happy to settle into what he calls 'comfortable sex.' I'm not." To Rebecca, frequency is the symptom, not the problem. She thinks their sex life isn't intense enough. She has tried to solve it by taking vacations. She feels they do much better together away from everyday life. And she has developed an active fantasy life that has David being much more adventurous sexually with her than he actually is. But her dependence on the fantasies started to make her worry that she wasn't emotionally connecting with David during sex, and so, ultimately, she went into therapy. What Rebecca found out was that "it was almost like I had developed an incest taboo about David and I had to remember that he wasn't my brother and it was okay to be sexually far out with him."

This is a problem for many long-term couples, especially for peer couples. They have the skills and desire to communicate, and they want intimacy and are comfortable and open with one another, but this can lead to low-key sex that makes passion seem out of place. As David said, "I feel tender toward Rebecca, love her, enjoy making love to her, but I have to make myself think of her as a sex object. I mean she's sexy, but she's not my sex object. She's my friend, and that's what's most often in my head about her. And sometimes it's a bit strange to get down and dirty with your friend, you know?" Rebecca is definitely fighting for her erotic life. She talks about moments that start to work well for them and then get lost because the more cerebral part of the relationship takes over. "I was really horny. I hadn't seen David for a weekend because I was out of town. We met for dinner and had a babysitter, and I know we were both feeling romantic. We started off holding hands, but then we started talking about the things that were going on in his job and amazing things in mine, and before I knew it, all those sexual feelings had gone out the window."

Peers like David and Rebecca suffer from sexual disinterest for three reasons. First, part of the problem for most of these couples is sheer habituation. Couples stop thinking of new ways to be together. Their sexual practices become predictable, regardless of whether they are still or were ever satisfying. Another more mundane reason for less sex is lack of care about personal appearance: friends don't dress up for one another—they expect acceptance and don't concentrate on physical characteristics. They may gain weight or forget personal hygiene at bedtime. They expect to be desired for their less "superficial" selves. Finally, some of these couples suffer from the inability to perform an essential transformation, a transformation from everyday identities to erotic ones. They can't let themselves go and give themselves over to the abandonment of everyday rules of conduct and personna that great sex requires.

So how do couples accomplish that? How do they bring the yin and yang, the principles of opposites and mystery, into a relationship that has been built on principles of sameness and openness? One answer for some of these couples is the creation of a separate erotic reality. They create a special sexual environment off-limits to the mundane aspects of their daily life.

Passion and the Creation of New Identities

When Sue and Gil interact with one another, the sexuality between them is palpable. It is surprisingly strong for a couple in their late forties who have been married for twenty-four years. Gil is tall, very thin, and very elegant. He is an architect and looks the part. Sue is a professional classical musician. She is on the short side, with an hourglass figure. She flirts with Gil in everyday conversation, and it is hard to believe that these traditional female maneuvers are absolutely separate from the governing dynamics of their relationship—but they are. Sue and Gil are each other's best friend; they spend as much time together as possible (although that can be scant, because Sue tours part of the year for her music), and there is no responsibility or decision they wouldn't be happy to take over from the other or to share. They really are an enviable couple for their peer dynamics and sexual success. Sue believes their secret is that she always thinks of Gil as a lover whom she will sneak away with as soon as the last guest leaves. "I think of him and myself as sexually dangerous—capable of anything—and therefore we have to keep ourselves very, very busy! Seriously, we are both physical, and daring, and intense, and we keep that focused on one another. That's probably one of the reasons we decided not to have kids—other than the fact that we like to travel so much and need to too—but it's because we shine our light on each other, and we make sure it doesn't get dull."

They work on dullness in ways both usual—vacations and special nights—and unusual. Gil explains, "We have black-tie dinners and dances where everyone comes looking gorgeous. We dress up for going out a lot. We work on our bodies. We shop for Sue's dress together. We are sexy with one another in the dress shop. We keep that look in our eye that way. We'd probably die if we were separated, but that doesn't mean we don't know that there are forces out there to do that, so we don't let it happen to us. We're too physical. It's too important."

Sue and Gil have invented a special sexual world they both inhabit. David was unconsciously speaking about his inability to create such a world when he said he had trouble having sex with Rebecca because it was "un-her" or "un-him." Men in sex therapy often talk about wanting to marry a "good" woman, but have passion only with a "bad" one. Both traditional and untraditional couples alike have trouble allowing each other new identities in the bedroom, but those in peer marriages have the most chance of surmounting such boundaries because they allow each partner more latitude.

For one person to be a spectacular performer in bed, it is necessary for the other to grant that person permission to become this new creature. "Granting" must be active, by showing extreme pleasure and arousal at this transformation. Sexual transformation is impossible if the partner steadfastly refuses to see anyone but the mother of his children or the earnest breadwinner in bed.

In traditional relationships, it is the man's responsibility to sculpt the woman's sexual self. A stereotypic and symbolic example might be a scene in a novel or movie in which the man takes off the woman's glasses or lets her hair down, thus releasing her theretofore unseen beautiful and erotic self. The man here is the teacher and discoverer. If this were a peer couple, either person could signal a release of mundane realities.

Rather than waiting for her husband's release of her erotic self, the wife in a peer marriage is more conscious about her independence. She is not likely to walk through her house door and abandon herself to become a creation of her husband's appetites. Her self is established by her full citizenship in and out of the household, and it is this security that gives her the freedom to experiment in bed; if the self is secure and hierarchy isn't present, innovation isn't threatening.

Cindy, who works with the weather service and the army, spends a lot of time in planes doing various kinds of research and is the only woman in her unit. She feels that her colleagues' respect for her is hard won. But when she gets back home and has intimate moments with her husband, she feels she can inhabit a different personna without losing any ground in her husband's eyes. "I don't think I have to worry about my femininity and my masculinity confusing Jack. He knows that when I'm doing weather recognisance, I'm one person, and that when we are rolling off the bed, I'm another—and yet I'm the same person. We have these serious impressive jobs, but we don't let it get between us and some cannon-firing orgasms. One of my favorite things to do is to come out of the bathroom with some slinky bodyslip on that he's never seen and walk up to him like the world's greatest slut. Oh yes. Me. And loving it. And him loving it. I let him take it off with his teeth. And, no, I don't worry about him asking me to cook just because I'm a terror in bed."

Cindy's ability to take on both identities, to transform at will, creates a sexual relationship that is not overwhelmed by her image as a daring and competent professional. If she worried about compromising her dignity or felt that one standard of conduct obviated the other, she couldn't create a new erotic reality. If she felt her dignity were imperiled by her sexual game playing, she couldn't do it. And dignity—or one's perception of what it takes to maintain it—can be an erotic assassin.

Today we swim in a sea of hypersexuality. We have adjusted our sights upward; basic performance is just not enough. The atrophy of passion that can afflict peer marriages is more of a catastrophe than it would have been in more innocent times. The sexual dilemma for all couples is how to keep at least some passion, sometimes alive. For peer couples, the answer is in the construction of separate sexual identities that allow them to escape the confines of everyday life without damaging the essential elements of equality that is the foundation of their relationship. It can be done. The elements seem to be the following:

1. Contexts are set up in which work and homelife identities are forbidden. Mundane conversations are avoided; parental and economic concerns are postponed.
2. Physical appearance is taken seriously. Feeling sexy sometimes requires sexy clothes or at least changing from everyday wear.
3. Identities in bed have nothing to do with identities out of bed. Sexual game playing has to be within each individual's emotional and political comfort level, but successful efforts to stretch those boundaries have erotic payoff.
4. Games of dominance and submission can be successfully played if those roles are traded back and forth over time.

5. Both partners take the responsibility to make sure that sex happens, that it happens the way each person needs it, and that it has not fallen into rote patterns. No one person can be blamed for a problem.

Mick and Darla are a peer couple who follow the rules and who feel that their sex life is never too familiar or familial. They have busy careers. Mick, age forty-four, works on a newspaper, and Darla, age forty, works at the state environmental office. With three children—two biological and a much younger adopted daughter—there is limited privacy and time. But it is clear they are strongly sexual with one another. Their success at sustaining a passionate marriage is based on maintaining their sexual life as both an extension of their equality and as a result of their commitment to keeping their sex life alive. Darla says her heart "still beats a little faster when I see him getting undressed and he gives me that kind of wicked look which means he's going to suggest something sexy. It's embarrassing to talk about all the things we do, but I'll tell you a little bit. We play scenes, and we switch roles. Sometimes I'm the doctor who seduces the patient; sometimes he is. Or sometimes we don't give ourselves actual labels, but we're acting out seducer and seduced or playboy or playgirl. Or sometimes it's just that I'm all over him right away or he acts possessed. We give each other complete freedom."

Mick clarifies that these ways of having sex together are not simply an accident: "I never want sex to be business as usual. I'd rather not do it. Occasionally, of course, it is, but never twice in a row. I don't want to get sloppy with one another. I have a horror vision in my head of this pot-bellied guy distractedly humping his wife who still has curlers in her hair. Not for me in this lifetime. We create a mood. We think of each other as sexy people. We never talk shop in the bedroom. If we talk about our work, which we do all the time, we keep it confined to downstairs. And we do other little things as well, like wear nice things to bed, so that the removal is sexy. I want some drama. And we make sure nothing gets in the way of that."

Both people in this marriage are committed to keeping up their sex life, both are committed to looking good for one another, and equality pervades both planning and execution. Sexual imagery and satisfaction is predicated on cooperation rather than control. An intensity of feeling comes from the combined energy of two independent forces.

Arnie, age twenty-six, describes that feeling: "We don't do anything special. But it's looking into each other's eyes, long and hard, and just letting ourselves know that these two powerful persons are entering each other and that this special thing we are doing is special because we are special to one another. That's where the explosion comes from—all that combined power and love and pride. Because, you know, I really am proud of her, and that's part of the turn-on at these times."

Sexual transformation for these people is facilitated by both the creation of new identities and the thrill of their real selves. Transformation becomes especially difficult after the relationship has been established. It is not that once the mystery is gone it cannot be recreated; rather, when couples are exceptionally intimate and known to each other, there is often the temptation to be consistent with the person one is thought to be. If a person enters the relationship with a sexually wild personna, it is easy enough to insist on its continuance. If one wants to invent it post hoc, the truly new aspects of the self unsettle the previous assumption of full personality disclosure.

The possibility of sexual transcendence through new identities is burdened by past experience, both sexual and nonsexual. The repertoire of selves developed with earlier spouses or lovers may be either richly diverse or stultified. Moreover, moral compunctions act as constraints. Certain identities, such as being respectful to the opposite sex, are not lightly transcended. Both men and women are often afraid that if they experiment with who they are in bed, the rest of their personality will crumble and their relationship may founder. Feminists and other women who have fought hard to be taken seriously worry about lurking frailties or gender patterns that might slyly set them back. Being rough during sex or using explicit language and falling into traditional masculine and feminine roles may be threatening to some women; it is hard for them to embrace these acts as liberating. If they are to enter the raptures of creative sex, the political climate of the marriage has to be so secure that these specters can be overcome.

Intense sex can be ratified by the couple as a mutual transcendence of everyday life. An additional intimacy emanates from knowing that only the couple has seen this aspect of each other; only they know what the other person is capable of. This additional knowledge adds to their deep friendship rather than betrays it.

The Coordination of Two Autonomous Sexual Appetites

One of the major sexual hurdles of any relationship is finding a sexual style that suits both partners equally well. Men and women have trouble decoding each other's sexual signals, a dilemma traditionally solved by men doing what they want and women adapting. Peer men and women, however, recognize each person's right to have a particular taste and need, and so once the right to an autonomous sexual appetite is granted, the coordination and satisfying of those appetites is something of a challenge.

The more equal a couple is, the more each person is careful to respect the other's desires by taking on appropriate responsibilities. Each person has the equal right and also the equal responsibility to initiate or refuse sex. When there are no leadership responsibilities, confusion or resentment may surface as one or the other person takes the initiatory role. Traditional asymmetrical sexual scripts have their drawbacks, but they did have the advantage of clarity. Egalitarian couples now face the trade-off between equality and coordination. Women are unaccustomed to taking responsibility for making sex happen. Most have initiated sex in their lifetime, few have seen it as a duty. Furthermore, neither they nor their partners are emotionally prepared for a lack of sexual interest on the male's part. Men are supposed to have an ever-present sex drive; lack of interest is hard for women to accept without insult. Both the man and the woman may feel that a lack of response connotes physiological failure, role failure, or a problem with the relationship.

Sexual response has to be established by negotiation and conversation. Because most women learn something about their sexuality before marriage, they will come to this relationship with certain information about what they want. How it works in any particular couple is where the art of sex occurs. Some guidelines from peer couples follow.

First, there is no rule that says the man has to be sexually hungrier. Appetite is an individual characteristic. Peer couples get used to the idea that the woman might want sex more often than the man and that says nothing about his or her masculinity, his or her femininity.

Second, the person with the greater appetite has the greater responsibility to make sex happen. If this happens to be the female, she has to overcome past proscriptions and taboos. She needs to see the refusal as part of her partner's sexual personality rather than a rejection. If the man is hungrier, his partner needs to accept his more frequent initiation as personal preference rather than dominating behavior. And partners must take care to allow the less interested person the chance to initiate. Sex must be a responsibility of both parties.

Third, because men in traditional relationships usually have sex on their erotic schedule, they are sometimes surprised to discover that they can be uninterested when sex is suggested by the other person. Men discover that their sexual appetite, like women's, is situational and not always responsive to someone else's mood. In the beginning of egalitarian relationships, some men found sexual demands upsetting. They felt, as women have, that their partner's attempts at seduction during moments of strong disinterest were annoying. Peer men learn to refuse with goodwill and sensitivity, much like women of goodwill have learned. One peer husband recounted how nonplussed he was one night when his wife turned to him and said, "I want to make love to you. Turn over please." His reaction was "to seize up rather than turn on." He wasn't used to taking the traditional female responsive role; he didn't know how to respond to a sexual overture when he hadn't been thinking of sex at all.

Fourth, since the very nature of autonomous sexual appetites means that peak coincidence is rare, peer couples use their intuitive skills to gauge how interested a person is even if they are essentially receptive. And any care taken to increase the chance of mutual interest (having sex when the children are fast asleep or after an affectionate "date" together) helps ensure that sex will be highly attractive to both partners.

Fifth, because initiation and refusal duties and privileges are shared, the frequency of sex and even the themes of sex may be different from previous relationships. If the man no longer feels compelled to initiate a lot of sex and the woman is not so hungry that she takes up the slack, there might be less sex than among traditional couples. If the couple has found the right amount of sex for them this way, lesser frequency should not be upsetting. Peer couples, like other couples, can have high, low, or medium sexual frequencies. What is important is that each person is getting the chance to have an equal voice in what happens and that it is negotiated in a mutually satisfactory way.

Sixth, there can be more innovation. Equalizing the initiation and leadership responsibilities doubles the creativity that can be brought to bear. Many peer couples speak of this.

The Specter of Extramarital Sex

It wouldn't be a bad bet to suppose that a disproportionate number of all the words ever written about sex concern extramarital sex. One of the great fears of marriage throughout history has been the loss of marital fidelity. In the United States, survey after survey has shown extraordinary unanimity about the centrality of monogamy to marriage. Most surveys show at least 85 percent of both men and women feel that monogamy defines marriage and sex outside the marriage is a betrayal of marital vows.[11]

In modern Western marriage, premarital sexuality for women has become something of a matter of course, but monogamy in marriage is no less sacrosanct than ever. Whether traditional or egalitarian, it is the rare couple who wants an open marriage that allows extramarital liaisons; most couples feel strongly that intimacy and trust require sexual exclusivity as well as emotional fidelity.

We do not have data available to know whether marital affairs are more or less common in peer marriages. On the other hand, modern times might seem to lead to more affairs. The workplace now is the largest meeting place of men and women, and working conditions often require long and intimate relationships with the opposite sex. Premarital sexuality is much greater than before, and research shows that postmarital sexuality, both faithful and unfaithful, correlates with it.[12] Both single and married women, who used to have lower outlets of all sexual acts than men, now demonstrate, at least in some studies, equal ability to be sexually adventurous, break rules, and seek partners from workplace associates. On the other hand, affairs have always happened, they are never well measured, and the foregoing conditions are not specific to peers.

What we can discuss here, albeit a bit more theoretically than empirically, are the various causes of infidelity in traditional versus peer marriage and resources available to cope with it. Among traditional couples, much of the risk lies in the possibilities for anger and for boredom. The research on nonmonogamous women shows that they are either looking for some playful, ratifying experience long missing in their relationship, or they are angry and lonely and seeking a way out of the relationship or at least a way to get some kind of hidden revenge for past mistreatment or emotional abandonment.[13] Men are also capable of having sex for these reasons, but they are less likely to be looking for romance and more likely to be tempted because of sexual or emotional inadequacies in the marriage. A larger number of men than women will have recreational sex if they have the opportunity. And some men will hire prostitutes to give them an act they cannot get at home or have an exciting evening without, as they see it, putting their marriage in jeopardy.[14] However, regardless of difference in motivation, the number of men and women who have sex outside the marriage and treat it lightly is small.

From this perspective peer marriage is not only less likely to create the conditions for unfaithfulness; it is perhaps a cure for them. That is, in fact, the origin of Holly and Seth's reconfiguration of their marriage. They were married about five years when Holly felt suffocated by Seth's tight management of family finances, travel, decorating, and future plans. She loved Seth, but she resented him, and she began to feel that he didn't respect her enough. Seth traveled extensively for his work and didn't bother to check in much. Holly began to feel set free, and she didn't realize how angry she was at his controlling style. One night she was out drinking with three woman friends, and some men asked if they could sit with them. Two of the other women were single, so they invited the men to join them. Holly started bantering with one of the men, and after a couple of drinks it seemed like a good idea to go back to his hotel room with him. Drunk as she was, she knew what she was doing; her only fear was that the man, a total stranger, might be dangerous. He turned out to be a perfectly orderly sort of fellow, even suggesting and providing condoms. She said her only regret that night was that she "couldn't stay longer."

The next day, she felt terrible guilt. She came from a religious background, and while she didn't attend church regularly, she went and confessed her evening to a priest. Then she felt she had to deal with Seth because it was apparent to her that her actions were fired by anger and disillusionment with the marriage. When Seth came home, she told him what had happened. He was stunned, furious, and distraught, and he cried. Then he left the house, and Holly thought the relationship might be over. After some stormy scenes, they decided to go to marriage counseling. Through counseling, the basis of their marriage changed. Seth stopped trying to be so dominant, and over the years, their marriage has come to be more equitable in Holly's eyes. Neither has had an outside sexual relationship since the incident they reported ten years prior to the interview.

This is not to suggest that peer marriages are invulnerable. Indeed, the passion problem can combine with the pull of traditional eroticism to lead partners to seek traditional affairs as an erotic supplement to their friendship relations with each other. Peers, however, have more resources for confronting these situations. Jay and Bernice were married twenty-three years when Jay had an affair that threw their relationship into turmoil. Both psychotherapists, they would have said that they were invulnerable to sexual midlife crises. But Jay succumbed to his emotions about an attractive young psychologist he met while teaching part time at the university. Jay is astounded at his behavior: "I was the last person in the world you'd ever think would do this. It never crossed my mind, literally. I just didn't think about such things. I would tish-tish with Bernice when we'd hear about one of our friends being unfaithful, and I thought it was tacky behavior. Then I met Mai. She was so bright and sparkling, and at first I thought my interest in her was completely platonic and academic. I like to be a mentor to students. I've worked with dozens of good students, and some of them, the women, were very attractive, but there was never any question. We started going out for lunch, and after a while I knew I found her attractive. But it was still innocent, because, well, I don't think of myself as a sexy guy, and it wouldn't occur to me that she would be sexually attracted to me. One day we were having lunch, and I don't remember exactly what the subject was, but it wasn't about us, and right in the middle of the sentence, she takes my hand and looks me straight in the eye and tells me how much she cares about me. I was incredibly flattered. It got heavy right there, and we went back to her place and had sex. After I got over the exhilaration, I had this incredible wave of guilt, but that did not stop me from seeing Mai. I was seeing her about twice a week and going crazy with guilt. I had never kept anything from Bernice before, not anything, and here I was leading this double life. It was really grinding on me. It got so I couldn't even be happy with Mai, because I knew it was wrong. Finally, I just couldn't bear it, and I came home one day, walked through the door, and told Bernice the truth."

Bernice was devastated: "I can't really express how awful it was. I just took it for granted that Jay and I had a wonderful marriage, that we had done everything right, and that we were solid and invulnerable. And to find out that he had held some other woman in his arms, had told some other woman his deepest feelings—it makes me sick to think about it even today."

Suddenly the entire basis of a peer marriage was at risk; the core concept of best friendship was threatened by hurting the other person but also by breaking the lines of communication and intimacy. Despite Jay's physical attraction to Mai, he didn't want to lose the truth and closeness that had been built up over so many years with Bernice and on which they had both relied. As much as he cared for Mai, he couldn't imagine as complete an integration with anyone else but Bernice, and when he had to face up to what he was doing and make a choice about who he was going to be with, he couldn't pick anyone but his wife. Jay explained, "You have to understand that even though I was becoming addicted to Mai, I was a mess because I missed Bernice. I would be with Mai, and in my most selfish moments, I wanted to call Bernice up and tell her, so that she could be happy for me! I didn't even think of Mai as a replacement for Bernice—Bernice is the other half of my spirit—but I never had this kind of excitement before and I was torn between horrible, horrible guilt and not wanting to give up this new feeling."

Jay was seduced by the passion of a new love and the passion of difference—of age, of experience, of attractiveness. Meanwhile, his sexual relationship with Bernice, like most other long-term sexual relationships, had mellowed into something comfortable and fulfilling but not passionate. They had watched it go from extremely nice to very pleasant and thought, as many other couples do, that that was the way it had to be. Because they felt bonded for life, a little loss of passion didn't seem a dangerous thing.

When Jay finally faced the truth, Bernice was heartbroken but said she could understand "how it could happen." She hadn't thought about their sex life very much. Their sensuality together centered around food and talk as much as anything else. She thought sex could continue on automatic pilot at this point in their lives. She was wrong. They couldn't turn a twenty-three-year marriage into a new affair, but they did have to stop treating their sex life as a residual, and they had to spend time reinforcing their friendship to see what wounds it had suffered through Jay's defection. They survived. And it was their peer strengths that pulled them through.

Extramarital sex is an easy but dangerous solution to the passion problem. Traditional and peer spouses may not know how starved for physical affection and confirmation they are until they suddenly bloom under the approving glance of a stranger or coworker. This is particularly true if partners have been extremely unattentive to one another's physical needs, ego, or desire for variation and romance. If they are attractive and personable, sooner or later some outside person will stir their hormones, if only by demonstrating attraction and sexual interest.

Another "solution" to the lure of passion is to deny its legitimacy and to extol companionate and comfortable sex. This is reasonable if neither partner has a huge sex drive or if there is no previous history of passion in this or other relationships to remind a person that sex used to be dramatically different. But for couples with a history of a mutually passionate relationship or with previously passionate relationships, too much downgrading of the importance of sex in the marriage might not work. "Comfy" sex is what most couples live with, and live with happily, most of the year. But some will rebel if it is all they will ever have. Having something to hope for, whether during vacation time, intentionally special moments, or random heightened erotic occasions, may make the difference between being satisfied with a long-term sexual life together and being vulnerable to other passions with other people.

The Rewards of Romance

There is, as the basis for love and commitment, a very old concept, imperfectly performed, but with an honorable history: companionate love, that is, romance that sustains because of the everyday rewards of mutual support, pleasure in togetherness, and easy affection. Eroticism may be necessary to fulfill some individuals' emotional needs, but all successful couples need some measure of companionate love.

Companionate love of the past was premised on gender restrictions. It functioned through a balanced exchange of emotional gifts and tasks that each sex presented within sex-role guidelines of what men and women are supposed to provide to one another. Romance was a junior partner to cooperation and loyalty in this admixture. Today, however, the expectations for companionship have increased exponentially, and romance is more important than ever before.

What is required for marriage to have the romance needed to sustain itself? First, peer couples demonstrate dedication to being a couple, over and besides being a family. Next, they display of physical and verbal affection, both because it is rewarding and also to distinguish the erotic nature of the couple from nonmarital best friends. Third, they spend time together that is nonutilitarian in purpose so that the couple continues to function as intimates as well as a partnership. Fourth, conversational exchange, gifts, and behavioral demonstrations show that the partner is more valued than other people. Fifth, and finally, celebrations of special days that mark the relationship's beginning, history, progress, and future renew intimacy.

All couples need these conditions to enjoy romance; in peer couples they seem likelier to occur since both partners take responsibility for them. Traditionally, many of these elements were in the wife's sphere: nonutilitarian conversation, displays of affection, and expressiveness. But releasing women from sole responsibility for this sphere has not allowed it to slip between the cracks. The opposite seems to be true: 90 percent of the couples interviewed said that both partners are good at memorializing dates, providing affection, talking about the relationship, giving gifts, and showing in word and deed how important the relationship is to them. In traditional marriage, when women do much or most of this work, the lack of reciprocity ultimately causes resentment and eventually attenuation of expressiveness. It may not disappear, but it becomes less frequent and less gracious. With peers, when more than one person has expressive skills and uses them, more positive exchange takes place, and the level of satisfaction is higher.[15]

Quite a few of the interviews showed how equality and equity produce a higher quality of romance. Carol and Buddy are a second marriage. Both had extremely unsatisfying first marriages—Carol's so brief it was almost nonexistent, Buddy's not much longer but extremely traumatic because his wife was an alcoholic and verbally abusive. When they met each other at age twenty-six, they were pretty battered for such young people. They lived together before marrying, cautious that they might make another mistake. Their caution helped them set up a peer marriage. Neither had an ideology of feminism or equity, but each was nervous about being responsible for someone else; each wanted to make sure they had someone who was able to stand up for themselves, contribute to the relationship, and give as well as take.

From this cautious beginning, a generous and supportive relationship has evolved. Because both of them had felt starved for affection in their first marriage, they have been careful to keep up a high level of physical affection with one another. They hold hands, touch each other, and establish regular warm eye contact. They are clearly each other's primary audience. Once each year they take a two-week vacation together, in addition to shorter vacations with their children. They try to take a weekend together every other month if they can arrange it. They like small intimacies, like going to the farmers' market together; they think cooking together is sexy. They do not have sex more frequently than most other couples—about two or three times a month; they describe it as "nice" or "wonderful to be together." They nonetheless consider themselves to have one of the most romantic relationships they know of.

Kristin, age thirty-two, and Joseph, age twenty-nine, are very much dedicated to the peer marriage ideal. They were married while Kristin was in graduate school and Joseph was working in the computer industry. They are very much a team in the peer model; they do a good deal of palling around together, have many mutual interests, including the starting of their own computer repair and consulting business, and are dedicated to the centrality of romance and sex in their relationship. They dedicate their weekends to music; both of them play an instrument and support the local chamber music festival financially and as volunteers. They travel when their lives allow them. They have no intention of having children, partly because they want to keep their adult relationship central, romantic, and sexual. Both of them felt that their own parents had had more or less utilitarian relationships—not bad but not profound. And they have high ambitions for their own. They pay attention to how happy they are, almost on a weekly basis. Their main activity at home is intense conversation. Whether it is about movies, music, or friends, they spend hours and hours debating, rehashing, analyzing. Their sex life is frequent, varied, and occasionally passionate. What they marvel at is the level of romance they sustain.

Many of the couples interviewed for this book felt they had sustained romance according to their own high standards and expectations. Many had sex lives they felt proud of, and almost all felt their romantic lives were exceptional. Perhaps this is the highest of marital achievements. Peer couples continually ratify each other and the relationship by the respect and romance they give each other. They routinely provide for one another in the small, romantic ways of conversation and intimate relations. Passion can be invoked upon occasion; but what they are really superlative at is romance—the good and lasting romance of equals. Romance is the signature of a peer marriage, the prized marker of a sexual democracy.

— Chapter 4 —

Eliminating the Provider Role

The linchpin of marital inequality is the provider role—or, to be precise, the provider complex, a combination of roles that give the man the responsibility for financially supporting the family's life-style and the woman all the auxiliary duties that allow the man to devote himself to his work. This division of duties is elemental to traditional marriage; indeed, traditional marriage is defined by it. Even if a man is called on to do some child care and a woman must work outside the home to help the family live better, the real responsibilities of traditional couples are clearly differentiated according to male earning capacity and female caretaking.

The ideology of traditional marriage holds that each sphere has its own honor and power, with homemaking and child raising theoretically as elevated and as important as money making. Money making serves merely as support for the real and consequential outcomes of success: a good home, well-reared children, and a fulfilling life-style. Male and female combine forces to achieve this end, and each gets a vote about family life.

In reality, however, the person who makes the buck makes the

111

rules, or at least the key contested rules. If we could measure each partner's ability to get his or her own way, the provider would win. Research corroborates this belief. In *American Couples,* for example, Philip Blumstein and I found that decision making correlates with income: the person who makes more income has more decision-making power, and the more distance there is between incomes, the greater the control the high earner has.[1] Other studies have come to essentially the same conclusion.[2] Defenders of traditional marriage offer a corporate metaphor, with husband and wife as equal stock-holders, but the reality is quite different. Sometimes there is rather shocking evidence that the low- or nonearning spouse has few rights concerning even what might be considered essential and elementary family resources. For example, the author of a study of working-class families found that working class women systematically had less access to family cash and in fact lived less well than their husband. Women were less likely to have a car, less likely to eat the same amount as or as well as their husband, and less likely to have similar discretionary spending money or decision-making capacity.[3]

Female earnings, thriftiness, or contribution in kind (producing needed family items such as homemade clothes) are often desired or expected, but they are not seen as replacing or competing with the male right and responsibility to be the provider. Even if the wife has more money because of a job, or windfall, or inheritance, both her husband and she may feel it does not entitle her to power in the relationship. Unless both male and female believe that women are entitled to equal power in the relationship, her earning power will be circumvented or at least modified.[4] One traditional woman I interviewed who had inherited a vast sum of money did not control it independently, nor did she feel she had any particular right to control it more than her husband did. Quite the contrary. She felt that because the man was the provider and the economic head of the household, it was his responsibility to handle all serious economic matters. As soon as the wife received the money, she put it in a joint investment account that her husband controlled. One heiress said, "He's the financial person here. I think it would show a lack of confidence in him if I kept money separate. I think he would wonder if I was not totally committed to our marriage—which I am. I really hand over everything but petty cash, and I didn't think of this as any kind of different category than our other money."

Even women who consider themselves the family accountant do not necessarily view themselves as responsible for the financial well-being of the family. Many traditional women keep the family books, oversee investments, and control cash outlay. This work does give them some measure of power in economic decision making, but most of them serve as the family agent rather than as its CEO. They do not think of themselves as the provider or even coprovider; they think of themselves as a supportive team member.

Most women are not taught, formally or informally, to expect to be a provider. If they find themselves divorced or widowed and in charge of their own and their children's survival, they often feel a shocked sense of betrayal because this wasn't the way it was supposed to be. Even if they have been working, they are not prepared for the full weight of what the provider role really entails. They did not pick a job or make choices thinking that their salary or a salary they could earn would determine their life-style.

Despite high divorce rates and larger numbers of single mothers, modern married women are just starting to consider themselves as necessary contributors to the family economy—and yet they still do not consider themselves to be the person who is going to be blamed if the family doesn't do as well as expected. An increasing number of women are starting to earn the same as or more than their spouse, but for most of them, this is a happenstance that is good for life-style, not necessarily a role that is comfortable or welcomed. Women often resent being the more constant or higher earner. One lawyer I interviewed was upset because she had been made a partner in her firm before her husband was, and now he was considering leaving the job and taking a state job that paid a good deal less. She said, "I'm not ambivalent about my success; I'm thrilled. But I am highly ambivalent about Ray's thinking about dropping out—well, not actually dropping out but doing less than he's capable of doing. The idea of being the big earner is something I never really considered. I just assumed that it would be him or that maybe we would be both near equal. Now I can see where he doesn't have quite the drive that I do, and I find that unsettling. It's not a matter of money; it's a matter of me being the more responsible, the more necessary earner, and, honestly, I'm not completely comfortable with that."

Most men also feel uncomfortable with sharing or relinquishing the provider role. They have been socialized to provide for the family and have trouble reconceptualizing this responsibility. A man who loses his job or stagnates in a job that does not meet his financial expectations is troubled enough. When he cannot provide for his family and his wife *can*, a different sort of challenge to his self-concept arises. If this situation happens in a traditional marriage, with neither husband nor wife expecting an economic role reversal, it creates a crisis. The man will almost surely insist on remaining the main decision maker; however, the longer he fails to provide, the more defensive he may become about his right to be head of the family. Typically his wife will support his leadership for quite a while, perhaps indefinitely, but quite possibly his authority will erode once it becomes clear that he cannot fulfill the provider role. His wife may act less differentially, even if she is avoiding the full mantle of provider. He may become aware of the change, and his anger over his loss of status may make a volatile combination with her resentment and worry about being the high earner.

The ideology of the provider role traps traditional couples into an unequal set of standards of successful family functioning. But ideology is not the only way this role orients the relationship. The larger economic system makes the provider role hard to ignore or escape. The fact is that there are still more high-paying "male" jobs than female jobs. Near peers, couples who may start out trying to have a fairly egalitarian relationship, often find themselves sideswiped by the economic facts of the work force; if they want to get ahead, the best way to do so requires following the man's career possibilities, which might necessitate sacrificing the woman's potential success and earnings. The highest number of the highest-paying jobs still go to men. Even in professions that offer men and women very large salaries, such as medicine, the subspecialties that pay the most (e.g., brain surgeon, anesthesiologist) are still heavily male. In prestige professions, women are more likely to be lower on the status and pay ladder. In "pink-collar" jobs, women are usually in the nonunionized, more unstable, and less independent jobs. Many of them are jobs well worth leaving. In the pure service of economic self-interest, many couples who planned to work and stay "balanced" find themselves having to curtail one career to promote another. In the not-too-distant future, this tendency may strike men and women at random, but now the great majority of these decisions end up, sometimes quite unconsciously or reluctantly, putting the man in the provider role.

More often than not, the couple's plans for parenthood help make that decision. Women's attachment to the parenting role plays a part here, as does most couples' mutual intent for the woman to be the main parent. She is expected to stay home with the child anywhere from several months to many years, and she is the designated person for most child-related needs after she returns to work. If both the man and the woman agree that children are best served by being with their mother and that this philosophy requires an episodic relationship with the work world, then the man's role as the main wage earner becomes even more central. Both partners, in an effort to protect the family's central income, conspire not to interrupt or disadvantage the man's work; if a child is suddenly sick, the mother (or a mother surrogate) has to be available to take care of the child.

This arrangement can endure for years. A typical American has two children, and if the couple is financially able, the wife will stay home at least several years during each child's infancy and childhood. The majority of women return to work before their children are in kindergarten, but each woman's designation as primary caretaker modifies the possibility of her being the provider long after the children have left the home.

Given these attitudes and economic facts, it is hardly surprising that the provider role stays allocated to the man and that the provider complex results. Couples agree that it's the best arrangement and that they will deal with the consequences later.

Consequences of the Provider Role

Obedience

The provider role is not easy. It is in many ways a noble role. The man takes on the burden of family survival, and if he is lucky, or talented, or both, he can work hard to create a life-style for which his family is grateful and of which he is justifiably proud. The role is endless, though, because the husband can always provide better; he is never off the hook. Especially in countries like the United States that offer increasingly extraordinary consumer goods, elaborate houses and second homes, and electronic toys of fabulous capacities, no amount of money ever seems to be enough. Extremely high earners generally practice conspicuous consumption as proof of what they have achieved. Families with old money may merely need to use their name to get deference and respect, but more anonymous achievers tell the world who they are through their cars, clothes, and houses. Perhaps having a wife who does not need to work shows the world how great the provider truly is. The desire to have massive evidence of success drives workers ad infinitum to further achievements.

Doing one's best requires long days and evenings of work, times of worry and fear, and the danger of mental and physical exhaustion. Providers suffer and sacrifice to provide, and often they want something in return for this effort. At first what they want is appreciation; later they seek obedience.

Most traditional men and women would hardly put it in these terms. They might call it "support" or "holding up the other end of the household." But to be head of the household implies that all other household members hold a lower rank. And while a good and kind ruler should not incur resentment, occasionally the ruler will have to make unpopular decisions or unpopular requests. He might reason that his ability to keep the family going is dependent on the strength of his support services, so he does not think it unfair to get mad when those services seem inadequate. When the dry cleaning is not picked up, or a child or wife's schedule endangers a business commitment, the entire family (not just the provider) is at risk.

The price of the provider role isn't cheap. The more the provider provides or the harder he works to do so, the more he feels entitled to emotional returns and provision of services. One woman in a near-peer relationship complained, "Things have really changed since Max's promotion. When we were both struggling to get ahead, I'd say we both took care of the household pretty equally, and we were even more even on Elaine's [their daughter's] weekly stuff. But between what it took to get to VP and what it takes to maintain it, he palms off just about everything on me now. And what ticks me off most about that, is that unlike before, he doesn't feel at all guilty about it. He just expects me to do things he would feel apologetic about before." Another near-peer wife said, "I swore that I wouldn't be like my mother who was the only one in the household, including my father, who knew where my dad's clothes and underwear and things were. I mean he had no idea where his things were because he expected her to get them for him—and she did for maybe fifty years. She was the housewife, and she was supposed to do everything. He was entitled, you know. And somehow, creeping slowly up from nowhere, though it seems like it started almost against our wills, Pete has started to be more like your old-style husband, expecting everything to be done for him because he's so busy and important."

Economic Control, Psychological Backlash

Traditional marital wisdom has it that all money earned is family income. But interviews of traditional and near-peer marriages show that neither husband nor wife generally feels that way. Women who do not work or who earn much less income than their husbands feel constrained about acting independently with family money. Their fastidiousness is not shared by their husbands; many more men than women make big-ticket purchases without consulting their wife. They feel that the money is their's and they can spend it however they want. Even when there is precious little to begin with, sociologist Jan Pahl finds that, any discretionary income goes disproportionately to the male.[5]

A few traditional and near-peer wives try to retain a bit of control by keeping some separate money, but this is rarely a considerable sum unless the couple is quite well off. The ideology of marriage includes commitment to pooling money; keeping separate money implies incomplete commitment. About 80 percent of all married couples pool their money and resources.[6] At first glance, this might seem to be a far better deal for the wife than for the husband—she gets more than otherwise, and he loses some control over his earnings. Yet if we assume that the male contribution to the pool is greater, his money renders hers virtually unnoticeable. He ends up directing the use of both sources of money.

Women who have husbands who make extraordinary sums of money may live well and have so much discretionary income that their ability to spend freely is never questioned. Yet they too can be severely constrained if they exceed their husband's opinion about how much money should be available. Sometimes these controls are never noticed amid lush circumstances, unless the marriage runs into trouble and dissolves. Many wives at all income levels, but especially those who were very well off, are shocked to find out what their husband feels they are entitled to (or not entitled to) when the marriage ends. The checking account is closed, the charge cards withdrawn and the amount of money available is predicated on very different premises than existed throughout the marriage. The traditional wife or lower-earning near peer spends pretty much at the pleasure of her husband, as a matter of his generosity and delight in enacting the provider role.

Many wives are aware that if their husband no longer wished to share the bounty with them, they would be in economic peril. This compromises more than an occasional unhappy wife's ability to leave her relationship. And it is an unspoken fear in even well-functioning marriages. Women who are economically controlled and deeply dependent cannot help being a bit afraid of a life without their provider. This cannot help but severely compromise how they act in their relationship.

Even so, the provider complex is a bargain that many women are happy to make. They either do not wish to be a provider or do not believe they could be one if they tried. They may voice serious resentment when their husband is stingy, untrusting, too controlling, or merely less generous than they think is appropriate yet do not generally clamor for an end to the provider role. They would like the provider's privileges to erode, and they would like more shared control and respect, but women who have neither been prepared for the provider role nor taught to want to provide approach it with caution and, often, fear and distaste.

With this lack of enthusiasm for change, it may seem not only impertinent but foolhardy to champion the cause of the minority fraction of couples who do away with this role to be peers. And it would be foolhardy and even cruel to encourage everyone to eliminate the provider role if marital contracts were enforced for life. As bad as the resentment gets and as controlling as the husband might be, many women are content to have less status, power, and respect as long as they and their children are economically supported.

But as the notion of equality spreads, resentments of the provider complex are hard to avoid; they build and build and start to undermine the harmony of the household. They bring emotional conflict and feelings of unfairness that buckle the foundation of the marriage. Tensions over cooperation and respect that are displaced by the provider complex can lead to the end of a marriage, with the wife at risk of being absolutely destitute and certainly much poorer. Divorce will cause an economically dependent woman to drop class status like an elevator cut from its cable.

The traditional wife in a provider complex may do everything she can to maintain the relationship, to the applause of conservatives, who believe that economic dependency will slow the divorce rate. This stance ignores two problems. First, even traditional women will take only so much, especially now that equality is so widely embraced. To the extent that the provider role works against modern women's requirements for love and fairness, marriages will be troubled. When a woman's lack of independence causes her to be a supplicant in her own marriage, honesty will be undermined, along with the emotional directness that helps marriages mature and become more intimate.

Second, for marriages that are abusive, the conservative scenario is a cruel one. If the wife is unable to provide for herself and is in a dysfunctional relationship, she may stay married well beyond what is in her own or the children's best interests. Dependency may force her to stay in a marriage in which her own and the children's lives are endangered.

Economic dependency can cause dishonesty between spouses. Countless housewives, or lower-earning nonpeer wives, resent the fact that their contribution is not appreciated, and they feel they deserve more than they get. They are part of a partnership and should share equally in the profits and the decision making. But they do not feel strong enough or secure enough to insist on a new economic deal. So what do they do? They open up a secret bank account or save up money for the spending their husband might not approve of. This "mad money" is testament to the fact that they think they cannot be an equal partner in deciding the way family money should be spent, saved, or gifted.

Quite a few traditional women I have interviewed have a private discretionary fund that their husband knew nothing about. Even more common—perhaps almost universal—is that they told him that items cost more than they did—and they kept the difference. Husbands often hear fictitious price tags because women are not full partners and do not have the right to buy at the level they feel is appropriate. The more traditional the relationship is, the less likely it is that the husband shops and has occasion to know what prices really are, and the less likely he is to question her quotations.

Sometimes her hoarding of cash is not for herself. One traditional woman told me, "I keep money back so that I can do for the children. He has this idea that they have to have the same childhood he had. I can't make him see how old-fashioned that is. So I keep some back, and I give them the allowance that their friends get." These wives give little gifts of money to the children that the husband would not approve of, and they collude with their children to keep the information secret so that the system can continue. As long as the money never enters a joint fund, the husband doesn't realize that a shadow economy operates in his own household.

Affluent wives use another way of getting around economic dependency: They fight their insecurity or reward themselves for various insults or services with a frenzy of consumer energy. They go shopping not as a utilitarian exercise but as a way to feel good, as a way of punishing their husband, or as a way, sometimes unconsciously computed, of feeling that they are getting as good a deal as they are giving.

These strategies have other than economic costs to the relationship. They encourage deceit and dishonesty, erode the capacity for deep friendship, and institutionalize resentment. If the husband finds out, there may be anger, or patronizing acceptance, or perhaps pain and confusion about why his wife would not be honest with him. Two traditional husbands have told me they know about their wive's "little extravagances and caches." These upper-middle-class men felt bemused, superior, and paternalistic. They *expected* their wives to "skim a little off the top" and were rather proud that it could be done without economic injury to the household. But it hardly promoted mutual respect between the partners. This example leads to the next consequence of the provider complex: its effect on husbands' respect for their wives.

Male Lack of Respect and Ingratitude

Because the provider role polarizes men and women, it inevitably, albeit indirectly, causes a loss of respect for women in their husbands' eyes. Men appreciate traditional female skills but don't respect those services as much as they say they do. Even significant economic contribution doesn't get a woman as much credit as she thinks she is getting. Studies have shown that women who work may think they are making a great contribution to the welfare of the family and may believe that their husband feels the same way. Men, however, rate the wife's work as less important than their own and as less of a contribution than the wife does.[7]

Both men and women consider the provider role difficult and demanding. Feelings and fears about responsibility are accepted as a major burden for the provider. It is this ultimate responsibility, beneath all surface issues, that husbands and wives admire and credit. All other labor, while appreciated, is seen as less onerous. No accumulation of effort ever seems to outmatch the provider's contribution. Husbands and wives typically agree that child care is hard and important work, but the fact is that it is considered just a part of a woman's duties, whereas the provider role is deemed to be all-consuming for the man. The message is consistent: Only the provider role releases a person from auxiliary labor.

The traditional and near-peer men in this study consistently underestimated the effort that goes into household work. Certainly someone who has never shopped for children's clothes or spent the day running around doing small errands may have difficulty believing how busy and time-consuming a day is when "nothing important gets done." Most of the middle- and upper-middle-class traditional and near-peer men interviewed believe at some level that wives have an enviable life, with more freedom and less anxiety than they have. Quite a few said that they wish they could have that life—but seemed to say so more for the interviewer's benefit than to express a true desire. When asked, "Why not try it?" the answer was that they could not afford it. Peer husbands, by contrast, did not think about household chores in economic terms. Many actually enjoy these tasks. Like many wives, they like to cook, take pride in their homes—or at least some part of the cleaning or homemaking experience—and can think of only a few duties that they wish they could hire someone else to do. A comparison between peer husbands and other husbands on the subject of household tasks shows how little respect and how much avoidance traditional husbands display toward these duties.

Credit is more likely to be given in an area in which the husband has somewhat more participation in, such as child rearing. But even here credit is modified by how difficult he believes child raising to be, and how much he enjoys the subtleties of raising children. The proof of his regard is how much time he gives to his children and how much else he expects his wife to do. Only a few of the traditional husbands interviewed felt guilty about their working wife's double schedule. They did not see the "second shift" as inequitable because they did not think it was as difficult as she made it out to be. The provider believes that nothing is quite as hard as being the provider, so even when he thinks his wife is burdened by a second shift of work, he does not see her as being any more burdened than he is.

Wives are upset about this situation. Although some studies have shown that women who believe in the provider role feel that the load of household and child-related duties they carry is equitable, others have found that the weight of underappreciation and overload of responsibilities is hard on women.[8] Most wives who are part of the provider complex feel that they rather selflessly perform their myriad duties. Like the provider's job, their own work is never done, can always be done better, and carries with it high expectations. There is some compensation, of course, since women have been raised to take care of others; many love to cook and clean, and others take satisfaction in knowing that they are talented homemakers and caretakers. They can do without fair credit for their contribution—up to a point. They can bear being taken for granted when they receive some respect. When they do not, they become angry and unhappy even if they don't believe their bargain can, or should, be changed.

Traditional women want appreciation and help. What they get ranges anywhere from temporary aid to a husband who is furious that his wife doesn't just do her job and shut up. In some homes, this rage can be an excuse for violence. A recent study showed that the most common argument preceding wife battering was about housework.[9] The homemaking role is a surrogate for the wife's display of obedience to and support of the husband, and any crack the violent husband sees in that picture can drive an angry and insecure man to a physical attack, an attack that puts the not-quite-low-enough wife reassuringly further down.

Most wives receive a far less destructive reaction to their performance of homemaking tasks, but that does not mean they like their treatment. Most wives have bitter complaints—sometimes cloaked in humor, sometimes just hurt and mad. A traditional wife who has been married twenty-five years says that her husband's expectations and complaints still make her angry: "When he complains that the towels aren't folded just so, it just drives me wild. He doesn't understand any disorder in the household. He thinks that making sure that two teenagers fold towels is a test of competent motherhood or something, and I simply can't stand when he does that sort of thing." A wife in a near-peer relationship is furious; she and her husband return home from work at about the same time, and he is upset when dinner is not well thought out, ready relatively quickly, or, most important, "hot": "We have continual dialogue about the importance of a hot meal with all the basic food groups. No, I'm not kidding. It's not enough I get something on the table; it has to be well balanced and eye-pleasing. Meanwhile, I am also supposed to pick up the cleaning on the way home and things like that which he will help with if he can, but if he can't, I'm supposed to. It's like he will help, he will cook, he will pick up, and he will menu plan if he can—but he doesn't understand what it is as a responsibility, day in and day out. He does his thing and thinks he's about equal. But he's nothing of the sort. And it is almost worse than nothing at all because then he thinks it gives him the right to complain all the time about his three food groups!"

Hundreds of behavioral science studies show that men do significantly less work in the household than women do—and not because of income, opportunity, or even employment.[10] One study showed that the *more* women made relative to their husbands, the *more* housework the wife did! The author concluded that women who suddenly earned more than their husbands were deviating so badly from their traditional role that they were madly compensating by doing reassuringly feminine work. Their husbands, embarrassingly cut off from their usual validation, shied away from the housework that a more secure, high-earning husband could afford to do without further damage to his masculinity.[11]

Whether women are earning more, less, or the same, the ideology of the provider sets up women to do "women's work" and men to "help." Men have specific boundaries. Their province usually includes heavy lifting, car maintenance, and lawn-related duties—work that can be done sporadically, perhaps over the weekend. This separate sphere operates even when it is quite clear that doing the job together would be a bonding experience that would help create the family attachment they both say they want. For example, one traditional couple both looked at me in amazement when I suggested that the exhausted new mother should ask her husband to share the nighttime shift with the baby. "Oh, no," she protested. "He couldn't do that. He needs his sleep for work. I can afford to be exhausted. He can't."

Distortion of Men as Partners and Persons

The provider role is an elemental part of how both the male and female rate the man's competence as a partner. Only couples with a drastically different approach to marriage are able to separate a man's worth from his paycheck. Peer men and women try to do it. The black couples I interviewed were most likely to make this distinction, particularly because both husband and wife saw black men as systematically excluded from opportunity through no fault of their own. But these are the exceptions to the rule. Most men and women see a man, his worth, and his work as intertwined.

This is a fragile base for a marriage since the role can be disrupted by outside forces. The economy can go sour, or physical disability can occur, or jobs dry up in a specific sector of the work force—or a man turns out not to be as talented or as successful in his chosen line of work as he, or his wife, thought he would be. If the provider role is a huge part of the husband's status and worth in the relationship, the marriage cannot avoid being devastated by the long-term inability of the husband to perform that role according to expectations.

Even if the man is doing well, expectations may rise higher than his earnings. Just as men are often unreasonable about giving credit for women's roles because they know little about them, women can be extremely demanding about what kind of income generation is possible because they do not understand the vagaries of the economic market the husband struggles to succeed in. Even if the woman does know that "it's a jungle out there," her view of the possible and the necessary is shaded because she is not demanding the same thing from herself that she asks from her husband. She may be content to work, for example, for a medium salary in a job without higher earning potential. But she expects much more from her husband, and she is prepared to be a much harder judge of him than of herself because she and he have a different mandate. Over time, especially as he is drawn away from the family by the demands of his job, her focus on his adequacy increasingly narrows to the provider role.

The provider role both remains prioritized and is taken for granted. People tend to concentrate on what they don't have rather than on what they have. While both husband and wife have agreed that the husband should be mostly unconstrained in his pursuit of income, once that is not in jeopardy, women tend to take the maintenance of family life seriously. Almost all modern women want their spouse to be their friend, to be knowledgeable and active in the children's lives, to be romantic and communicative in the marriage, and to have shared leisure time with the family. Sooner or later, these expectations and desires are compromised by the pursuit of the provider role because the more dedicated the man is to being a good provider, the more it is likely that he will falter in his family and marital duties. Neither the husband nor the wife may know how much work activities could be cut back without endangering the family's income, and this ambiguity of risk makes it hard for men to make rational decisions about how much of himself can be given back to the family at any given time. It is also true that the better a provider he is, the more likely he enjoys his role and the world he lives in while doing that role. He may not want to be with the family as much as the family, or his wife, wants to be with him. If his wife does not have a job that competes for her emotions and time in the same way his job does, she will channel more of her self into family situations. Women are mostly unsympathetic about the auxiliary effects of men's attachment to the provider role—their desire to be among co-workers, in "optional" work or work-related activities, especially if those activities consume precious time that the family has to preserve carefully if family members are going to have time together.

The outcome is that traditional and near-peer women are in a catch-22. The provider role is duly emphasized, so much so that the man's adequacy as a partner rests on his fulfillment of his wife's expectations. But at the same time, it is seen as a drain and competitor for the family and marriage's needs and time. The difficulty of successfully orchestrating both the provider role and the family and marital role is rarely rationally analyzed. And the thought of deemphasizing the role as an answer to the conflict is all too rare.

Peer Marriage as a Remedy to the Provider Complex

People seek an egalitarian relationship because they want fair treatment, respect, and the right to have equal voice in creating and maintaining a fulfilling marriage. In addition, since the organizing principle of peer marriage is that partners should be best friends, they need to know each other's life and needs well and be able to cooperate without psychological or any other kind of hierarchy. In practical terms, these requirements rule out the provider complex. But more than pragmatics is at issue; this question goes to the definition of marriage. Peer couples are evaluating marriage according to the quality and type of time spent together; they are reinterpreting marriage.

Peer men and women came to reject the provider idea from a variety of experiences. Some come from marriages that failed due to provider-complex pressures on their marital esteem. Some realize that they cannot "have it all" if "all" means maximum income with devoted motherhood and parenthood. But however it happens, the elimination of the provider role represents a fundamental rethinking of marriage, success, and partnership.

How do they do it? What are the costs? From my interviews, I believe that there are some common principles that have to be established in order to subvert the provider complex. Sooner or later, these steps have to be taken. The first step is an ideological one.

Reconceptualizing the Goods to Be Provided

One of the easy ways near peers derail their hopes of an egalitarian relationship is their entrancement with goals that lead to the provider role. If the man is financially successful, the wife gives up all previous demands for his time and cooperation and releases him to as much success as he can provide for them. Peer marriage is different. In order for peers to share economic responsibility and shun the provider role, they must put the marriage *above* their economic success. Couples emphasize the joys of making a good home, as well as the rewards of treating the family economy as a true partnership. It can happen with both persons working—with each doing their fair share and with no expectations that one person is more responsible for family financial success than the other—or with one person working, if each spouse has equal claim to money, its deployment, and overall economic decision making.

Even in my relatively small sample, the scarcity of couples with a nonworking spouse tells us something about how hard it is to get rid of the provider role when only one partner is providing. On the other hand, the fact that there *were* a few—and that some of the others had experienced a period when only one partner worked—means that dual careers or two workers are not essential to peer marriage. More important is the desire to reconceptualize the goods that a marriage provides, achieving wealth and security not as primary goals but rather as by-products of a joint home and work life. If deep friendship and cooperation are the goals, achieved through a system of shared governance, shared responsibilities, and collective ownership, then careers and homes will be designed to sustain, not subvert, peer marriage. Marriage is elevated to its most lofty, most ambitious possibility: a partnership for love and understanding, not a support system for childbearing or male careers.

In the reformed marital model, no one gets all the credit or all the blame for financial success or failure. No one is exempt from child raising or household tasks. Although the division of labor, like income, may not be precisely equal, it is not greatly unbalanced. No partner takes a disinterested or uninvolved relationship to the other's territory. There does not need to be a purely androgenous household in which sex role characteristics disappear, but the collaborative nature of the relationship ensures that each person will be strongly represented in the important elements of the couple's everyday life. Perhaps the best way to illustrate some of these modifications of the provider role is to describe a few couples who have done it.

POLLY AND GREG

Polly and Greg hold a strong commitment to equality, but for very different reasons. Polly, age forty-seven, was an active feminist in the 1970s, traveling this path because she abhorred her parents' quite traditional marriage and vowed that she would rather be single than be dependent. Her father, a well-to-do businessman, had run the family, and her mother almost always obeyed him without question. If there was a conflict, Polly remembered her mother backing down, always supporting her husband when there was a public disagreement over child-related issues. When Polly was older, she chided her mother for her continual acquiescence, and when her mother defended the hierarchical organization of their household, Polly was both sad and furious. She resolved to have a career and never to be subservient to a husband.

Greg, on the other hand, had never given much thought to feminist issues even though he was the same age as Polly and had watched the feminist movement grow on his college campus. The angry debates had never moved him much; he had grown up in an egalitarian household, and so the urgency of the feminists' cause was lost on him. His father and mother were artists, each represented by different galleries and both achieving regional success. Greg would never have called himself a feminist, but it would never have occurred to him to want a traditional wife or expect traditional wifely services. He assumed his wife would work and be his equal; he assumed that everyone would pitch in on household work and pick up after himself or herself. When he met Polly, her desires for maintaining separate control over money, for respecting each other's work and work demands, and for taking a mutual approach to solving everyday issues seemed a natural way to go about a marriage. He found some of Polly's anger about these issues justified, and they looked at some of the traditional relationships of their friends as unfortunate.

When they started out their marriage, Greg was finishing architecture school and Polly was in law school. They were both ambitious, and everything looked good for their future career success. In fact, both became successful. Greg became a principal in a firm that designed airports all over the world, and Polly was made a partner in her law firm. Both worked long hours and were rarely home, a situation that suited them until they decided to have children. They had two children in two years—and even a well-organized combination of preschool and help from the local college couldn't compensate for the loss of the time they had for each other and the chaotic nature of almost every single day. They could afford the expenses that came with living a good life based on their considerable joint income, but they began to realize how little they were together, how much of their life was handed over to hired caretakers, and how more and more responsibility was subtly accruing to Polly as Greg's business travel grew, and it became impossible for him to share equally in family maintenance. Worse, Polly and Greg were getting on each other's nerves.

Finally, in a series of intense debates, they put everything on the table: her job and how much she liked it and how much income it brought in; his job, and its costs and benefits. They considered how well they wanted to live and the cost of that life-style; then they examined how much they could modify their existing standard of living and still be content with it. The result was a carefully considered compromise. They realized that since Polly was a partner in her firm, she had more flexibility than Greg's work would probably ever allow, so they mutually agreed that Greg would be the person to modify his career. He left his firm and opened a small, mostly one-man architecture operation with hired consultants for specific projects. The first few years, he lost money; during this time, they relied on Polly's relatively high income. Over the next decade, however, Greg's practice grew to a respectable amount of work. Neither he nor Polly had any illusions that it would pay as much as his other job had—high-paying jobs in architecture are few and far between—but the change saved their peer marriage.

They have never regretted their choice. In fact, Polly has been thinking of following suit and joining a smaller firm, with even more leeway in her workday. The impact of lowering the intensity of their work has been, in both their opinions, "an amazing salvation of our lives." Greg says, "I was not only making lots of trips, but I would be gone for weeks at a time. That was fine before I was a father, but when Polly and I started raising a family, I knew there was no way I could stay in that firm. She and I worried about trashing my career. The money was great, I was on a fast track, and it was the kind of work I loved. But Polly and I weren't going to have one of these marriages where nobody sees each other and Polly would have to be making up for all the things I didn't have time to do."

Neither Greg nor Polly feels that Greg has lost status in the relationship. Occasionally Polly will make the "provider mistake" of presuming Greg can do things for the household that she cannot and too many requests and expectations start stacking up, but then Greg will say something and work will get reassigned. Greg also feels that being around the house more has made him enjoy certain kinds of household tasks. He feels more connected to his home and realizes that the flexible time and his more limited ambitions give him the time to be a more complete person: "Now my work gives me flexible hours. Even though I still work maybe fifty hours a week, these are *my* fifty hours. Except for a few meetings a week, I can do my work where I want to. When I worked at my old firm, I could never get away when I wanted to, even if it was important. For example, when Heather fell and hurt herself at day care, they called Polly to come take her for X rays. Polly couldn't be reached, so they called me, and, of course, I said I'd be right down. I went to one of the guys in the office and told him why I had to cancel our meeting, and he acted like I was from Mars. These guys have wives who take orders, and they don't respect me when I tell them my wife has a career too and she doesn't do all the stuff. It's not that I felt I was going to be fired for taking care of my kids. I just didn't like feeling guilty or pressured because I was trying to carry my share of the load in our family."

Polly and Greg knew that when he backed away from the provider role and they decided to share the economic and household responsibilities of their family, they weren't going to get unanimous support for it. Greg's family was horrified. They were proud of his achievements, and they couldn't believe he was "throwing it all away." Polly's mother and father felt she was being selfish and that Greg would always regret his choice and resent her for her part in it. Polly's mother also thought that Polly should have been the one to take less time with her work and allow her husband to shine. Friends were a bit more supportive, but Polly could tell that few of them felt at ease about their lowering their economic ability and changing the direction of Greg's career.

Greg and Polly never have regretted their decision, or ideological tectonic shift. They came to realize that economic success and old-fashioned providing were not as important as maintaining their family and their relationship. Even Polly, who once was driven by a feminist's need to prove herself as a provider, now is most interested in making sure that she and Greg safeguard their marriage: "I try never to lose sight of what this life is all about. You can get caught up and so excited about your own success that it is easy to get a warped view of what's important. But you need to step away from it, and you realize that the only thing enduring is the people you love. I've caught myself cursing that I have to go to a school meeting, not because I don't like them but because I wanted to finish some work. Then if I'm thinking clearly, I get my priorities straight and say, 'Screw the office.' I want to be there for Heather."   •

The fact that Greg had to curtail his career raises a disturbing general point. There may be some jobs that simply *do not allow* for peer marriages. Can an associate in a high-powered law firm, for example, be a peer spouse, while she or he must bill enough hours to be made a partner? In other professions as well, employees are expected to put in years of working long hours to prove their value to the company. Some corporations ask their managers to move almost every year and take several different overseas assignments in quick succession. The schedules of many medical specialties allow almost no personal time. Eventually the whole family may gain prestige, security, and money, and future prospects may be glamorous and exciting. But the price is dear. The job holder is unable to have the kind of flexibility and time that allows for parenting or daily shared experiences. The career runs the relationship. Occasionally, the job holder becomes so successful and powerful that he or she can change the job to fit family and personal goals, but by that time, the family may be grown up. Or, just as likely, by the time a person *can* change the system, he or she *doesn't want* to. By this time, the person has created a way of life and may no longer desire additional time with his or her partner or children. By choosing a job that is hostile or indifferent to personal relationships, a person unconsciously shapes his or her future possibilities for intimacy.

Greg and Polly consciously evolved a joint stance on how jobs and family intertwine. They are aware that the way they live in their marriage makes quite a few friends and colleagues uncomfortable. In fact, during interviews with traditional and near peers, I found that most couples believe that what Polly and Greg are doing can't be done. Both the men and the women worry that they won't be able to live with the psychological or economic ramifications of treating both partners as responsible in all parts of the couple's life. They also sometimes complain that they don't want a two-career life-style but that single-career couples are unequal by definition. Angie and Garrett are an example to the contrary.

ANGIE AND GARRETT

Angie has never had a paying job since she graduated from college. She came from a poor and chaotic family in which no one was ever available to help her or her sisters when they needed someone, and she swore that when she married, she would stay home and give her children what they needed. On the other hand, she is strong, intelligent, and independent, and she didn't want to be in a marriage that defined staying home as being a stereotypically junior partner in a relationship.

Fortunately she met Garrett, who wanted a total partnership, who was happy to have a wife who stayed home, but who did not feel that having a homemaker wife gave him any special exemptions from the duties of family life. He had grown up in a family with a nonworking mother who was a strong and admired presence in the household. Garrett modeled himself on his intellectually acute and emotionally intense mother and hated his father's oppressive treatment of her. When he looked for a wife, he sought out someone with his mother's strength and vowed not to be a husband in his father's image.

From the beginning, he and Angie shared everyday duties. He went to graduate school while she stayed home with the first of their four children, yet he helped every day with their care. When he joined a research institute, he gave her control of what he absolutely believed to be their mutually held money. When he inherited some family money, that arrangement continued. There has never been a moment in the marriage that they did not counsel together about decisions. And there has never been a time when he believed the money he made to be more his than hers.

In the beginning of the marriage, Angie had a bit more trouble feeling that the money really was hers as much as his. But because they talked a lot and she had everyday control over it, it soon became a mutual responsibility. When Garrett lost his job because of the merger of his institute with another institution, there was no change in how they operated together. They decided to live in reduced circumstances rather than leave their city and take another opportunity, because they both felt that they had established a community and friends worth keeping. They were thrifty and could live decently with Garrett doing occasional consulting. Their emphasis was on their needs as a couple and a family, not on his career or their money.

If anything, money had a bit of a dirty feel to Garrett. His father was constantly giving himself a great deal of credit for being a breadwinner, and he harped on its importance, to the point that Garrett became rebellious. Because he identified with his mother more than his father, he found no dishonor in homemaking, and he copied her fastidiousness as a house cleaner and home organizer. He never developed a knack for cooking but became a superior cleaner and took great pride in his home. Even when he was working full time, he was a full partner in raising the children. He attended every school play, counseled their oldest son when he needed help, and participated in all the family conversations, an involvement that helped him feel that he knew his children as people and not just as their caretaker. He loved Angie, respected her opinions, and was highly sensitive to any dismissal of her from professional men or women. To Garrett, the only marriage worth having is one to a peer; he wanted to be neither oppressed nor oppressor, and he felt lucky to have found a way to have a family that didn't follow in the footsteps of a model that he had never liked and that he knew would never fit him.

SELMA AND MARCO

Angie's and Garrett's willingness to live in reduced circumstances showed the seriousness of their commitment to the marriage and their evaluation of the provider complex. For Selma and Marco, the devaluing of the provider role proceeded and supplanted any desire to make a lot of money. Marco is a young man who wants to be a poet. He is married to Selma, who at age twenty-seven is two years older than he is. Selma is a massage therapist, and they live on an island within commuting distance of a city where she gets occasional work. They are caretakers for a doctor's weekend/summer place, which covers their rent, utilities, plus a small salary for Marco's gardening and handyman job.

Both have college educations; Marco has a teaching credential. But each feels strongly about having a life that revolves around internal satisfaction rather than jobs. Selma says they "are both spiritual people. We both spend time being in nature, meditating, keeping physically strong and in touch with ourselves. We've tried to do this in the city, but it defeats us, so it limits our options. We like being unattached to ownership, to things. We think that things keep you attached to things, and people keep you attached to people."

Right now it is Marco's job as a handyman that keeps a roof over their heads, but they both feel that at any time, the other person could be the one who is more responsible or successful at providing. Providing is not a valued role to them; economics is just a way to protect their combined freedom.

Neither of them enjoys home maintenance very much. They keep their house as minimal as possible and save their money to go on major hikes and outdoor trips. They don't expect much household labor from each other.

They have not had children yet, and they are a little afraid to do so. Both like children, but they are attached to their freedom from creating the kind of income they think might be necessary if they have a child. They go back and forth on the issue; their compromise now is to wait two years and see if they are ready then. They have no doubt, however, that when they do have children, they will take equal control of parenting, just as they have shared everything else in their marriage.

MARLENE AND DENNIS

Marlene and Dennis are outstanding specimens of the yuppie genus. They are in their early thirties and live in a fancy downtown condo. They can afford it because Dennis has been a successful real estate broker, and Marlene does management seminars all over the country. Both have high salaries, although Dennis usually earns more. Dennis met Marlene after a brief, disastrous first marriage.

Dennis was already successful when he met his first wife. He was only in his late twenties but had already bought and sold several expensive properties, and he and his wife started their life together renting an expensive apartment and living what he thought was the life of the beautiful people. His first wife was a hairdresser, and they were constantly invited to fancy parties where people dressed to the hilt—and where drugs were common. He found out that his wife was addicted to cocaine when some very unpleasant characters presented him with a massive unpaid bill. He paid and then tried to get his wife some help with her addiction. It didn't work, and after what he refers to as the "most ghastly years of my life," the marriage ended.

By the time Dennis met and married Marlene, he was financially cautious. He was afraid that too much money floating around was going to cause some horrible excess to take over their life. He didn't have to worry, for Marlene was as thrifty as he was; but she resented the controls he put on the money, the accounting procedures he invoked almost daily, and her sense that she was not trusted to be a full, vested, and responsible partner. She knew the details of his first marriage and was sympathetic, but she wanted full equity in the relationship or no relationship at all.

Dennis came to realize that if he wanted his marriage to last, he had to relinquish his control and instead trust Marlene and the relationship. Eventually they became coproviders, a relationship that required a lot of independence. They kept joint and separate books—sometimes they found out what the other person had made only at tax time—but they kept track of the general economics of their life almost weekly.

Working out an economic bargain helped them with other emotional negotiations. When they decided to have a child, Marlene wanted to make sure that she could slow down without losing her status as a full partner in the marriage; she also wanted him to slow down a bit too. The change was almost impossible. As Marlene said, "We were both A types—tough, on the go, just want to get in as much as we can. So we knew we weren't going to turn into Ma and Pa over this. But I did want to make sure that Dennis wasn't going to disappear and change this relationship into something that wouldn't make me as happy as we've been up to this point."

Dennis loved his work and wasn't ready to modify it much, but more than anything else, he did not want a divorce. Neither of them cut back as much as less compulsively active people might, but they made concessions. They spent more time alone rather than with clients. They made time to do some of the things at home they never had done before. They made a decision to invest wholly in the condo rather than continuing to rent. They made sure that the baby went to both offices, not just one, and that both absorbed the costs for running the household and child care. Marlene spent more time with their child than Dennis did, and her income went down when she stopped traveling as much. But they took care not to hand over the provider role to Dennis, and both of them feel that while their relationship is not the same as before, the most important part, their partnership, is intact.

From Ideology to Practice: Controlling Money Together

As these examples show, attitude is far more important than any specific strategy. Nonetheless, some practical suggestions are possible, the most important of which is to control money as a team. This sounds like a traditional approach except that traditional couples do not act truly corporately as peers must. Some of Garrett and Angie's friends subtly (and not so subtly) told Garrett that he was a fool for not acting like a breadwinner. Garrett said, "When we have dinner parties and Angie speaks up very aggressively about how we're going to plan the future or what car we're going to buy, I get the distinct feeling— and I know she does too—that in some way, she's not supposed to be so unreverential to me. I think most people think it is the man's money, or maybe just that it's the person's money who made it, and they don't like the kind of power and interdependence Angie and I share. You know, I even see this with couples in which both partners work—maybe especially from them. I think some of those women don't think Angie deserves to talk aggressively about, say, how much money we will or won't give Adam at school, because she doesn't make that money. Well, we don't see it that way—never have. Its *our* money. Even our kids had to learn that."

One path to co-management of finances was through experience. Several individuals had suffered financial fiascos in their past that changed forever the way they approached family money. Nina was one of them. She trusted her first husband to take care of everything: insurance, savings, and investments. When he died at a young age from a heart attack, she found out that he was underinsured, that he had made poor investments for which she was personally liable, and that their savings were minimal. It took her years to dig out of the mess she found herself in. When she and Burke became serious about each other, she insisted on being a full economic partner in their marriage. Burke did not agree. He was a stockbroker and felt that he understood much more about money than she did and it was ridiculous for her not to trust him to make good decisions. They almost broke up, but eventually he came to understand that nothing less than full partnership would make her feel comfortable and respected in the marriage. In this case, only the women's intransigence could break down the provider tradition. If Burke had not been able to change, Nina would have broken up with him, and it was only that level of seriousness and commitment to her feelings about money that caused Burke to change. He said, "If I could have made her see the wisdom of my point of view, I would have. I mean I thought she was a real idiot about this, and we really fought about it. But I saw that this was going to be it if I didn't try it her way. And I guess the bottom line was I didn't want to lose her. So I didn't—and I guess it taught me a few things. For one thing, I think she was right. This is a much better way to go about things."

Keeping Private Money

Joint management of joint money is essential. But autonomy for each member is also important. Most people want some privacy and some independence of action. When finances are tight, independence becomes hard, or even impossible, and conflict occurs often because decisions with no good solution available have to be made all the time. The ability to do some private spending is symbolically and practically important, especially for women. Having separate money is one way partners feel that they still have a separate identity, that they have not so merged that they cannot find themselves. Some peer women designed their marriages precisely in order to make sure they did not lose their identity, to make sure they did not "dwindle into wives." These women have a recurring nightmare that one day they will yield just a little too much—do a little too much housework or day care—and find themselves a junior partner in a subordinate position. By maintaining some financial autonomy, they assuage those fears.

Some peer couples, in an effort to give each other leeway and a vote of confidence, keep at least some of their money separate. Sometimes they deposit all of it separately. Seven of the couples I interviewed kept their money completely separate, with varying strategies for common expenses. Most had a house account they both put money into. Others casually tried to cover their share: Whoever went shopping paid, or one person covered the utilities and another the mortgage, for example.

Judy and Kenny kept everything separate because Judy was afraid of being trapped again in a relationship like her first marriage. She described her first husband as "a control freak" who doled out money in such small sums that she was constantly having to ask him for more. She found this situation debasing. And because her father was similarly controlling of her mother, for some time she felt that she would never be able to find a man who was not "a petty dictator." But Kenny, a high school teacher, had no intention of being either petty or a dictator. He met Judy at the school where they both taught, and from the beginning, their relationship was easy and friendly. When they moved in together, he respected her desire for independence, although sometimes he felt upset that she thought he would dominate her if they pooled their money. But since they both made about the same amount of money, it was easy to keep their finances separate and collaborative. Over the years, they accumulated enough money to buy a house together, but even then, Judy insisted on drawing up the purchase as a business arrangement. Finally, some fifteen years into the relationship, Judy felt comfortable enough that she lost track of who owned what. Still, she liked keeping separate accounts, explaining, "I think that one of the secrets to our relationship is the fact that we don't have to check in with one another about most money issues. We can disagree, we can spend money differently, and we don't get into it. I am just so glad not to be one of those wives that has to say,

'Oh, I'll have to ask Harold about that.' I just could not have borne that in my marriage."

Kenny agrees that keeping private money has helped their relationship: "There are quite a few arguments I think we've missed because we didn't know we had them!" In a more serious vein he said, "I don't think any one person should control money. I never really wanted to. I would have done it because that's the way I learned it. My dad was a bookkeeper, and I just naturally thought the man kept track of all the money. But, honestly, it was a relief to be able to share everything."

Sharing Worlds

Eliminating the provider role requires more than just using money equitably; it requires sharing each other's tasks such that mutual respect is naturally encouraged. Sharing such mundane activities as doing the marketing, or taking the children for shoes is the way to understand the importance of these acts, both for the family and as acts of solidarity with each other. Polly always gets home late, so there is no time during the week for her to do any housework or shopping. But Greg doesn't want to end up doing it all just because he is home, and Polly does not want to put him into the role of househusband, so they wait until the weekend or the occasional late shopping nights. And they do it together, which both see as companionable, well-spent time. There is some backsliding: Greg likes to do outdoor work more than almost any other household work, and he will try to trade it for less welcome tasks. He hated to iron so much that Polly finally took it over and reduced their ironing needs by about 75 percent by buying clothes that do not need pressing. But Polly's biggest gripe—and a common one among peer wives—is that Greg still likes to turn her into the guardian of who does what. She says, "I don't like to be the one who's always making sure we share the 'woman's work.' After all these years together, Greg still doesn't have a household executive's mind for noticing what has to be done—or at least not to my standards." Still, all in all, Polly is grateful and happy about Greg's household participation, which is one of the reasons Greg is happy to do it: "I get a lot of credit for everything I do—a lot from Polly's woman friends, a lot from her, of course. I'm sort of the local house hero. I actually find housework kind of soothing. I like having a clean counter;

I positively glow when all the laundry is folded! [He laughs.] Seriously, it can be very satisfying. And I wouldn't feel good if I wasn't doing these things as part of handling our life."

Another peer husband put it this way: "A grim job isn't so grim if you do it together. We're both lazy—but why should only I get away with it? And you know, if you do, you know it. And if you keep getting away with it, you stop being guilty, and you start to feel you're owed that. And soon it's like something you would never do. I think that's an easy way to lose respect for the person you've put it over on."

A Final Admonition: No Larger-Than-Life Players

When you sack the quarterback, you demoralize the team because you have hit at the heart of its ability to play the game. When you sack the provider complex, you strike at the heart of marital hierarchy and also strike down the single most elemental aspect of traditional marriage. This sort of change requires revising not only the relations but also the values of the spouses. One newly elevated value is respect. Peer marriage makes it almost impossible to operate as unfairly as before. There is no one who can command the head-of-household role and hold it individually and absolutely. Polly's father always wanted the family to acknowledge their indebtedness to his largesse: "He found it necessary to remind us maybe daily about how much he was doing for us. He was very generous with material things, and he thought that covered all his responsibilities to us. I never felt that way. Not only did I get tired of his telling us what he had done for us lately, slaving at the office, but I would have gladly taken more time with him instead of us having a new car every year."

Getting rid of the provider role removes the main earner's need—and authority—to demand hosannas for his labor and puts both spouses in the same game. Couples devalue the provider role's mandate for continuing success; in return, they get back family time. Couples who share the provider ambition and go full steam ahead may at least do it together and are not living parallel lives; but there are pitfalls for those who choose to solve the provider dilemma by encouraging full-tilt accomplishment by both partners. Two real problems can emerge: No one is left for household tasks, and the provider role may encourage competition between the partners. Neither is an unsolvable problem, but both are important enough to discuss here.

The Challenge of Competition

Being the provider encourages a "master of the universe" mentality; conversely, being provided for may infantilize the consuming partner. What the provider role does not do is encourage competition between partners. One of the strengths of dividing labor into distinct gender categories is that both spouses can be excellent in their area of accomplishment, and they will be absolutely uncomparable to each other. It is possible that one reason more *pairs* of doctors or lawyers or corporate executives did not show up in this sample of peer marriages is that spouses in these professions were more likely to run their relationship according to more traditional rules—or that the senior earner made so much money, and needed so much work time, that equality and collaboration were unlikely. It is also possible that two ambitious people in similar and competitive fields make conflict more likely—and break-ups more common.

While several peer couples had a business together, worked in the same field, or even shared a firm or practice and were convinced this strengthened their relationship, interviews with other couples showed tensions caused by competition. For example, Lynn and Roger met in medical school on the East Coast. They were both extremely talented and successful; she went into academic medicine and began to get all kinds of honors and job offers, while he ran a more conventional medical practice. His income was much higher than hers; her reputation was far greater. It became increasingly clear to her that he was jealous of the attention she received. When she was offered a prestigious speaking tour to Africa and then shortly after to Latin America, he became increasingly sarcastic and distant. At the time of the interview, the marriage was obviously in trouble. She was going to counseling, but he would not go after the first session, and she felt that the marriage was probably not going to last. She was very committed to her work, very disappointed in Roger, and very worried that no matter what men said, they could not handle a successful and busy woman who did not cater to their ego.

Another couple, also doctors who volunteered for the study, were similarly defeated by competition but in a different way. Wesley and Margaret also met in medical school. They were the stars of the school and graduated number one and two in the class. She was number one.

Both had intended to be surgeons, but he felt that they would never see each other if she pursued that specialty, so she went into internal medicine because she felt she could control her hours better. Over the years, he made a lot of money, and they were able to afford a luxurious life-style. He wanted her to be able to travel more and kept urging her to work part time, and finally she did, both because of his urging and her own sense that shorter hours would be good for her and their child. She said she needed the "opportunity to get out from the extreme pressure I was feeling, and take some time for myself. I'm not going to look back at these years and regret that I missed important events in my kid's life."

She did not feel that her husband was competitive with her personally, but she did feel he had become competitive for her time and resented her work because she was not free when he was. He had started devaluing what she could contribute at the clinic versus what she owed to her home and family. Still, she thought she had made a good choice in terms of her family and her marriage. Nevertheless, as she talked about her marriage and this new bargain in it, it seemed clear that she no longer approached the relationship on equal terms. When she talked about an extravagant purchase, she said, "Last time we went to Dallas, Wesley said I could spend $500 on a pair of boots, which we both knew was outrageous." She meant to be talking about some of the fun they were having together but a phrase like "Wesley said I could . . ." indicates a loss of peer status. When a spouse talks about the other's giving permission for anything, something very important has been lost. Margaret may have saved her marriage by changing her career, but it is not clear whether she got the life—or relationship—she wanted. Whether the competition between a husband and wife is a direct clash of egos or merely competition over how much of each other they will have, it has to be solved in a way that keeps equality intact.

The Challenge of Emotional Contribution

In traditional relationships, the division of labor is clear. Part of the woman's assignment is the emotional health of the family and the marriage. She is trained for it. From early on, little girls learn how to be "nice," to be acutely aware of the feelings of others, and to be a caretaker. They are more likely than boys to have babysitting experience, to learn how to cook and to clean—in short, to learn the homemaking and interpersonal skills that make them attractive as partners.

When the provider role is shared, considerably less time is available for caretaking, and the conditions of the work world often distract women from their instincts to nurture and caretake. The experiences of employment may also mute previous characteristics; being a manager or an employee requires an additional layer of skin. Not everyone is nice or fair or friendly. Workers learn that many, perhaps most, of the people they work with do not care about them and that kindnesses may not be reciprocated or appreciated. They may even be seen as a sign of weakness. People who work outside the home get a little tougher because they have to.

The combination of learning survival skills and not having the time or presence of mind to caretake can reduce the general level of emotional sharing in a marriage. Although women have now experienced several decades of work force culture and success in an often impersonal though not necessarily impartial workplace, men have had considerable less practice at taking up their share of the emotional work at home. Even the most well-meaning man may find that his wife feels he is not coming up with his share of the emotional labor that she and the children require and that she is providing to him.

If the couple has time together and if the man spends a lot of time with his children, some of these skills will develop naturally. But if the couple is in a fast-track world, both being intense coproviders, the chance that the male will be an adequate contributor to the emotional well-being of the household is small. Like any other group of skills, intuition, thinking of someone's else's needs, sensing their state of mind, remembering important dates and anniversaries, attending to the children's psychological comfort—all take time to learn and practice to perfect. Coproviders run severe risks if they think that these skills are any less essential to the success of their relationship than economic contribution, or if they think that emotional work somehow will get done in the tiny bits of time they allot for interpersonal interaction. In a traditional relationship, almost all of this emotional work rests on the woman's capabilities. The relationship rises or falls with her skill at keeping everyone communicating, interacting, and feeling good about themselves and others. Theoretically, a peer couple will have two people who can do this for the marriage and for the family. Theoretically, everyone in a peer marriage household benefits from the additional expressive contributions of the husband.

In relaxed households, the peer husband who has taken time to be with the family and the wife who is not running as fast as she can provide emotional comfort and acuity. But the pitfall for the fast trackers is present and real.

Rosemary and Buck have a peer marriage but nearly lost what they set out to construct because they put the relationship on automatic pilot. Both were social workers in the mental health field, with demanding schedules. Both directed large programs and also worked with clients. They worked extraordinarily long days and felt that life and their relationship were good until their twelve-year-old son, David, started hanging out with teenagers who were always in trouble. These episodes scared Rosemary and Buck, and they realized that they had not been spending enough time with David or, it turned out, with each other to give the relationship the emotional balance and ballast that it needed. They had been putting all their emotional talent into their work and hardly any of it into the family. They decided to cut away the nonessentials of their jobs, designed after-school activities to do with David, including counseling, and started getting home in time for dinner. Buck said, "We had a real scare, a real come-to-Jesus moment. It was the time to figure out what we were about, where our priorities were. And there was no question. What we didn't realize is how we'd let our work overwhelm our family needs. It was awful, embarrassing, scary. Now I'm spending a lot more time just talking with David, with Rosemary, with everybody."

A Final Word

The provider role shapes a marriage. Traditional wives who do not work or who act as minor financial contributors and do not have equal economic control in the marriage may think they are full partners in the relationship, yet in conversation, their husbands dismiss them more or do not even refer to them. These wives are more likely to be permission seeking, more likely not to try to extend a strong voice beyond the agreed-upon parameters of their territory in the relationship. They may be given complete control over the children, or household expenses, or even culture and social life, but the man retains veto power. This is not to say there are not good and satisfying provider role relationships. Many couples who are in such relationships do not experience them as lacking anything; if they do sense deficiencies, they would not put the blame on the fact that the man is the provider. Nevertheless, any comparison of these marriages with those that avoid the provider complex, with husband and wife sharing economic and family responsibility, puts the differences between traditional and peer couples in dramatic perspective. The peers are partners. They talk more together. They talk about more subjects together. At their most successful, the men can talk "women's language": the language of people, children, daily duties, and emotional issues. The women can talk "men's talk"; they are full partners in financial planning, spending, keeping the family afloat, and making whatever economic compromises need to be made to bring priorities and finance together. Men in these relationships do not feel totally responsible for economic success. Men and women are more broadly evaluated. By eliminating the provider role and removing what has historically been our highest external definition of success, the couple reaches for idealism. Their real ambition is to be intimate, to create and be a best friend. Economic success cannot be used to justify the family or the marriage. These couples construct a fairer world and perhaps a harder test of love and character.

Peer spouses think of their economic and household collaboration as a major advance, something that makes them irreplaceable to each other. They are members of a team who need each other. And in today's world, the combination of need, valued contribution, and emotional connection is a solid foundation for a strong marriage.

— *Chapter 5* —

The Shared Child

W hen traditional and near-peer men and women explain why they think it is impossible to have an egalitarian marriage, they almost always say that the reason is children. However, their reasons differ. Traditional couples believe that women should be the primary caretakers; any other arrangement is not in the best interests of the child. Their convictions are based on their own observations about the greater ability of women to nurture, the greater training that women have to parent, the great desire that many women have to be at home with their children, and their feeling that children want and need their mothers more than they want and need their fathers. A forty-nine-year-old pediatrician, Isaac, said, "I think all this social engineering is bad for children. Children need their mothers, pure and simple. Fathers are just a pale substitute for mothers. Of course, you need their involvement, but everyday care is best handled by the women—they know it, and men know it, and the pediatrics profession knows it. Even though I think I have great talent with kids, I don't think I am a substitute for my wife. My wife is a talented woman, and I am sure she will do something after the kids are out of high school. But now we both feel that our family needs her right where she is."

Many traditional women, and even near peers who value equality, insist on the right of women to be home with their children and argue that not being home with their children would damage both mother and child. They are not against the father's being there, and they would like more of him. But they assume that economic realities drive this part of the marriage contract.

The difference between traditional and near-peer couples is that near peers lament that they feel undermined by the work world and the resulting inability of fathers to be with their children more. Quite a few said that if they could manage a way to spend more time with their children, they would. Some have tried and failed. Harvey, for example, was directed never to bring his baby to the office again. Formally and informally, he was told that one more "fatherly episode" and he could be in trouble. He said, "I couldn't afford that. I had to do well enough to get a good referral. I was angry, but this wasn't the time to be unemployed. The truth is that bosses don't care if you are a good person or a good father. They want you to be a good employee, and if you have to work weekends and nights to do it, that's what you are supposed to do. I can't tell you how many emergency orders I've been told to expedite so they are ready by 6 P.M. Sunday. They don't want to know about my weekends with my children."

It takes great will, desire, or some luck for fathers to take up at least 40 percent of the parenting job. Most couples desire equality but cannot—or will not—sacrifice male income or job prospects. Gabe and Olive, a couple in their early thirties, provide a good example. Gabe is a part owner of a manufacturing company that makes a car part. He works night and day at this venture. At the same time, he and Olive are raising three young children, age six and under. Both of them want another child. Olive and Gabe like to think of themselves as an egalitarian couple, and they volunteered for this study as such. Olive directs the auxiliary programs of the local art museum and loves her job. They felt each respects the other's work and shares decision making.

During the interview, it became clear that the children were almost completely Olive's responsibility. Not only did she take care of them; she was very possessive about her right to direct decisions about them. Gabe, who loved children in general and his in particular, rarely saw them in time for dinner but felt he made up for that time on weekends. Olive disagreed; although they enjoyed family outings on the weekends, she was in charge of them. As the discrepancies grew between the spouses' versions of the relationship, it became clear that Gabe and Olive are near peers, not true peers. Olive apologized for their division of parenting labor but said she thought it had to be that way for a while "because Gabe has to be putting all his time in the office. I hate it, but this is a new business. I guess I thought that by now it would be stable—or more stable— and that it wouldn't be so full of crises so Gabe would be at home more and helping more. But it just seems to be one thing after another, so I end up doing most of the children's responsibilities. I love that most of the time, but sometimes it's overwhelming. Last weekend, for example, Gabe, who had promised he wasn't going to work on weekends, had to go back to the office. And while he was gone, Suzie pushed our little one, Toddy, into the mirror, and he was cut and I was hysterical—and where was Gabe? I found him on the portable [telephone], but I was furious. You know, this wasn't the way it was supposed to be. But I guess it can't be helped for a while."

This couple wants more shared child raising but the man is needed elsewhere. If he is more involved at home, they think, the family income will drop too much. They may not agree with traditional couples that only women can parent or that only women have the right to stay home with the children, but once they accept the premise of the provider role, they see no way out of the traditional division of parenting labor.

How do peers escape this trap? The difference between near peers and peers is that the former believe that, given an imperfect world, they are making the best bargain for their family. Peers disagree so much so that they make sure that coparenting takes place. It is not just through the sheer luck of having flexible jobs; it is also through willingness to forgo higher salaries in order to accommodate child raising. Some peers are high achievers who have enough power to design their jobs to their own specifications or enough money to hire child care. But in general, far more peers are peers by will, not luck. Their determination comes both from what they want and from what they wish to avoid.

The Problems of Traditional Parenting

What are they escaping? At least some of the following.

Decreased Overall Relationship Satisfaction

Over the past twenty years, a number of studies have examined the impact of children on marital happiness. Universally, they have shown that children take a major toll on the relationship. Satisfaction dips shortly after the first child is born and dips a little more with each successive child. It starts to rise when the last child leaves home. Parents are not necessarily *un*happy, but they are *less* happy.[1] Among the hypothesized explanations of why happiness decreases are less sleep and subsequent fatigue upon the birth of a new child, less time together, less time for personal and sexual intimacy, more economic worries, child-rearing disagreements, and child-related crises.[2]

What these studies have *not* hypothesized is that for traditional couples, this is the beginning of divergent lives. Couples who used to share school stories, or work issues, or a busy social life stop because the wife is now primary caretaker and has a much different life from her husband. They share less; they do not need or want to talk about the same things any more; the pressures they each have intersect less. They may need to talk to someone else more than they need to talk to each other, and their days have a different rhythm.

Women's Resentment at Male Absence

Some would argue that divergent lives need not affect the relationship adversely, but interviews with traditional wives suggest otherwise. There are books full of wifely complaints and accusations about the absence of male parenting. These women are not usually even thinking about equality of parenting; they just want more help, more empathy, and more companionship for themselves and their children. Although women may grant a male absence, they never cut him as much slack as he takes. Moreover, if his absence is so taken for granted that he is regularly unavailable, serious problems arise when child-related emergencies occur.

Hazel, a traditional wife just turning forty, had never asked for her husband, Mitchell, to be equally involved with the children. Mitchell was a salesman, and he traveled a lot, sometimes including weekends. Over the years, Hazel's resentment grew. Then they started having a lot of trouble with their teenage daughter. She was in a relationship with a boy who had dropped out of school, and she would disappear for days at a time. Hazel put her feelings succinctly: "When he's not there when she needs him—when I need him—I hate him for it."

Hazel has supported Mitchell in his career, but it has been a source of constant aggravation between them. His contracts for heavy equipment usually require meetings that are hard to cancel. In hard times, he has to schedule many more meetings to keep sales up, and he resents her resentment since they both know that he cannot fully control his time. Over the years, he has missed birthdays, anniversaries, and now, most seriously to Hazel, school meetings and meetings with juvenile court. Sometimes she is so upset with him they go days without speaking.

Children's Unhappiness over an Absent Father

When children, especially young children, complain about father absence, the parents feel guilty and defensive. The mother must defend or excuse her husband. If she confronts him in front of the children, she betrays and undermines him. Haranguing him to be home more may not only be ineffective; it may alienate the husband from both wife and children.

The role of apologist wears on wives, and as children get older, they may be less likely to accept the apologies. Affluent families can sometimes ameliorate absence by hiring first-rate child care or by filling the child's day with lessons and activities that are exciting and fulfilling. Nevertheless, the children and father are less emotionally connected when the father is absent a lot.

The traditional result is a family in which the children revolve around the mother and consider the father an unknown or fearsome or irrelevent presence. The mother, if she is attentive, attains mythic proportion; she is venerated and loved with passionate loyalty. The father is resented. Many of the peer men I spoke to reacted to their own father deprivation, by swearing to do it differently. A twenty-five-year-old peer husband said, "My main objective in having an equal relationship was not to be the kind of father that I had. I want my kids to know me before they are adults. I want them to have experiences with me and have me know what is important to them. I want them to be able to talk to me. I want them to run to me if they hurt themselves. I want our conversations to be more than me telling them they could do better on a test or that I was disapointed they didn't make the team. I want to be all the things to my kids that my dad was not. I want us to have hugged many, many times and not just on birthdays or their wedding day.''

Father's Emotional Distance

A lot of ink has been spent trying to understand why so many fathers are willing to get divorced when they know they will have less access to their children and why, after divorce, so many cease to have contact at all. Much of this research has been sparked by the problem of inadequate or absent child support payments. But why does the larger issue of paternal disengagement exist to begin with?

Certainly a man who has had less day-to-day contact with his children is likely to be less intensely committed to them than would a man who has shared raising them. An interesting study by sociologist Diane Lye showed that divorce rates may be related to that level of interaction. She found that men with sons were much less likely to get divorced than men with daughters or men with only one son. The reason was because men were more knowledgeable about how to relate to boys and therefore enjoyed more activities with them; this relationship created more investment in the children and more attachment to the family as a whole. The men who did things with their children tended to do the things they were familiar with: sports, spectator sports, carpentry, camping, and so on. They were much more likely to do these activities with sons than daughters and as a consequence spent much more time with their sons. Lye hypothesized that a closer relationship created an emotional intensity that made it much harder to leave those children and therefore affected the divorce rate. She wondered whether there would be lower divorce rates in marriages with daughters if men felt comfortable doing these kinds of activities with their daughters. Or, perhaps, if they became more comfortable with a broader range of ways of relating, more family relationships would be strengthened.[3] Disentangling the causes of divorce is a daunting challenge, but Lye may be right that the traditional emotional distance of fathers has helped accelerate the divorce rate. Once divorce became more acceptable, fathers with few connections to their children were more willing to leave their marriages.

Mother Absorption

Traditional husbands are thrilled to hold their newborn baby—and also quite happy to turn over the care of the child to their wife. But they are not so happy when their wife becomes so absorbed in the new baby that they find themselves shut out. I write a column in *American Baby* magazine. One of the three or four most-asked questions concerns who gets attention. Women often admit they are totally immersed in the new baby and they would like their husband to understand rather than be upset. They feel under pressure from husbands who pout from neglect. Husbands ask when their wife is going to rejoin the marriage.

This is not a big problem if it ends within a few months, but if it continues, it is the beginning of the end of a certain kind of intimacy the couple shared before children. Both husbands and wives may mourn the loss, but wives do not see the children as the problem. They are more likely to blame the distance on either their own or their husband's daily life. As a near-peer husband said, "I like to think of Libby as my best friend, but these days I feel like the kids get the best of her. She is definitely more involved with them than me. I understand why, at an intellectual level. But I also feel that we've lost something we had, and I'd like to get it back. I don't want to have to wait sixteen years to do that."

Traditional wives may desire a traditional relationship precisely because they want this kind of absorption in their children. The traditional women interviewed for this book talked about the importance for young children to have the full attention of their mother. Many who work are hurt that they have to spend *any* time away from their children. They talk about guilt and longing and worry for their children's welfare. One traditional wife described her children as "the most satisfying, important, and rewarding thing in my whole life— that includes everything."

Whether some women love and need their children this much because they are designed that way by nature or whether they develop this kind of love for children because their satisfactions from men are so much less powerful, the disparate investment cannot help but affect the marital bond. If the couple prioritizes success at parenting and economic survival, they may believe in their individual contributions in different realms. But if the glue that holds the couple together is evaluated for its mutuality and deep friendship, then the wife's absorption threatens the very thing she most wants: the stability of a family that serves the best interests of her children.

Relationship Boredom

From paternal distance, to maternal absorption, to wifely or children's resentment, traditional parenting accentuates the differences and divergent interests of husbands and wives. These divergences can lead to the opposite of deep friendship: relationship boredom. Men who are not involved in their children's activities or day-to-day affairs may not be extremely interested in hearing about the ups and downs of their children's friendships or school politics or peer dress codes. Women whose joys and cares revolve around the discoveries and misadventures of young children may not enjoy hearing about office politics over and over again.

Dean, a high school history teacher, is terribly disappointed in his marriage for this reason. "When we met," he said, "we were both young teachers with the same goals. I was attracted to her because she was so good and because she was so serious about her work. We would talk for hours—and not only about school issues but about American history. We both loved the Civil War. We went to Manassas together, visited a lot of the battlefields, and we read this huge trilogy on the Civil War as a joint project. It was one of the best things about our relationship. After we had our first child, she quit work. And everything changed. She seems totally fulfilled being with our children. I was afraid to have Matthew, but I love kids too, and so I was torn between wanting another one and fear about what this was going to do to us. My worst fears were realized. She doesn't want to travel, she doesn't want to read as much; she just wraps her life around those kids. We've gone to counseling, and it changed things for about three weeks, but that's all. I am committed to her and my kids, but I have to tell you I am so disappointed in our marriage right now, and I'm just counting on the hope that after Matthew is in full-day kindergarten we can salvage our relationship."

The Terrible Consequence of Near-Peer Parenting: Disengagement from the Husband

Near-peer women often complain of feeling like single mothers. They have careers, and they raise their children virtually single-handedly. The great danger of such a situation is that if the man totally cedes major, and most minor, child management to the wife, and if it is economically feasible, some wives in troubled marriages may start to wonder what they would lose if they left the relationship.

Near-peer women develop many skills, from learning how to check their car oil, to handling medical crises. After a long succession of these learning situations, a cost-benefit ratio becomes very clear. If the man is a good provider or a satisfying friend or lover, that may make the bargain feel worth the work. But if he is minimally adequate or miserably failing in his traditional role, his lack of help around home and family becomes one more reason his wife can rethink her options. Milly, age forty-two and now in her second marriage, remarked how she came to this epiphany: "I had a day from hell. All the children were sick with the flu, and the basement had flooded, and I had to run up and down the stairs—bailing and medicating, medicating and bailing. By nightfall, I was totally exhausted, and I was just crying out of sheer fatigue. Nelson was on the road again, and I just thought that as long as I'm doing this all by myself, I might as well do it all by myself. This came out of left field for Nelson. You know he said, 'I didn't know you were unhappy.' And I said, 'That was the problem. You didn't know anything.'"

The Peer Approach

Peer couples may not have all these potential costs in mind when they make up their mind to share parenting, but there are some common themes in their dedication to a more shared experience. Many of the women were seeking to avoid isolation, minimize alienation from their husband, and yet maximize attention to their child (by maximizing their husband's parenting). About 20 percent were feminists looking for equal respect and felt they could never get it if child raising was their major role. More commonly, both parents had jobs that required time and effort and brought in necessary money. About half of the women in the study spontaneously mentioned that they wanted to avoid the trap of trying to be a superwoman; none wanted to be the only one in the household who carried two jobs. Almost every wife brought up, in one form or another, the idea of equity and fairness. None of the wives insisted that their husbands do exactly the same amount of child care they did, but they felt their husband had to do much more than make a token contribution.

The men tended to fall into two categories: men who were trying to repair wrenching tears in their own family past by being the fathers they never had and men who loved their wives and wanted to put a bargain together that was fair for them. A few wanted to replicate the particularly wonderful relationship that they had had with their own father. A few were feminists who wanted to be part of a genderless world that promotes individual and collective justice. Most significant, almost all of these men loved children and wanted to spend time with them. Only one of them saw child sharing as a cost he had to bear to be part of a relationship he wanted to be in. It is the common male desire to join in parenting that gives me the greatest hope for peer parenting. The separations of the past are hardly natural. Though parenting means changing diapers and cleaning spills, it is generally viewed much more favorably than not. But what does coparenting really mean?

The Need for Equity and the Tension Between Equity and Equality

Equality, as political philosophers tell us, is inefficient. To rely on everyone equally rather than according to individual talents is a slow and messy process. The problem for peer marriages is that children require tremendous energy. Children in dual-career households stretch couples' talents to the limit. How do they cope? They do *not* do it by sharing everything. Most of our couples felt that fifty-fifty equality was not a good way to conceptualize their arrangement. For example, Tim said, "We try to be fair and still not get trapped by our jobs to decide what fair is. First we took turns at being the primary parent. I took care of Corey when he was little, while Claire [his wife] took an intensive program in translation and got the degrees she needed for the work she wanted to do. And then she took book work instead of trial work, which she prefers, while I finished school. So she was the first in line. But finally we ran out of that stage of our life, and after a lot of experimenting, we felt we had to get somebody to help with the kids, even though we didn't believe in baby care before

Nelly came along. Now we play it day by day—who can take the kids today and who can do the doctor's appointment this week. And while I think we both know that Claire does more of it than me because she has more flexibility, we make sure we don't start leaning on her so much that I stop doing my fair share. She won't stand for it anyway! And I really don't want to do that."

Equality is easy to measure. Equity is far more elusive, and one person's definition of fair is often another person's definition of exploitation. How do you equate a day at the office doing humdrum work with a boss who is an idiot, with a day of household chores and a child who is colicky? How do you compare overtime with weekend chores and child caretaking? All couples with children have to mix equality with equity because of great disparities in relevant talent (for example, helping with math or soccer). There is no way to divide all child care precisely in half, to measure visits to the doctor equally, or to measure hours equally.

But we are suspicious of equity when it cannot reduce to a simple measurement along a single metric. Many women have tried equity but have found it necessary to return to the principle of equality. Maybe it is "fair" for a man to do hard labor and a woman to be at home with three small children, but the inequality involved will inevitably cause conflict in the relationship. Ultimately, most of the peer couples in this study found that sharing in the same coin became the reassurance the woman needed to feel that equity was being served. Ultimately, equity had to be mixed with equality.

This is an uneasy balancing act for most relationships. Equity seems so reasonable and so much more rational that equality. The whole theory of Nobel Prize winner Gary Becker's new household economics is that women and men will want to do their respective types of work because of efficiency and because of the economic structure of men's versus women's professions.[4] When a chore is easier for one person than the other, then the one who must work harder to get it done is likely to do it worse, to take more time, or to incur more psychic cost. Since this is the state of affairs for most household and child-raising tasks for most couples, there are strong and reasonable pressures to dispense with the burden of total equality.

Peer women fear the psychic costs of inequality more than anything else. Marsha, a secretary for a small legal practice, said, "I saw my mom just get smooshed by having five kids. And my dad was the biggest baby of them all. No way for this gal; I figured this out real early. Not me sitting there crying at four o'clock counting the time 'til my husband comes home, and then getting one-word answers to my questions. Everybody said it wouldn't work when I married Harmon because they thought no man was going to go along with my ideas of child raising and a marriage where everybody did everything. Well, it's fourteen year later, and they're all divorced and I'm here laughing."

The principle of equity needs modification because it is a fundamentally individualistic theory. The larger good of the relationship can get savaged in the effort to protect each person's individual rights. Individual rights are not even the most important consideration in the social nature of household life. The worst examples of individualism gone too far are cohabiting couples who do not have a long-term investment in each other and guard their independence for fear of exploitation. Cohabitors tend to keep a running tab on who owes whom, and their emotional individualism often follows this economics model.[5]

Peers tend to be flexible and approximate about hours and duties. It is only when flexibility takes on the hue of a traditional division of labor that the principle of equality is invoked. One of these peer wives said, "When I notice that I can't remember when was the last time he took our ten year old to get his braces checked, then I get on my high horse and throw a lot of stuff his way." Time and effort are not the only variables; certain acts are symbolically supercharged, and if they are delegated to the mother, they undermine the whole idea of shared parenting. Pat and Thalia made a solemn vow early in their relationship that their children would never have school plays without both parents in attendance, would never have school outings that included only mothers, and would not face important challenges like doctor's visits or entrance exams with only one supportive parent. Pat said, "I always wondered where my dad was—maybe fairer to say *who* he was. I would wait until he was asleep or away, and I would go through his things—his briefcase, his wallet, his albums from high school—just to find out the person he might be. He was so absent from my life, and I guess I thought I could find out who he was from his secret documents, from his own childhood. I got used to his absences from almost all the important days of my life, but I never got reconciled to the sheer mystery of the man."

A near-peer husband became emotionally upset talking about why he wanted to get back into his children's lives: "I do plan on changing this crazy schedule I'm on. I hate the fact that right now I make cameo appearances in my children's lives, and sometimes I can't even do that. When I was out of town for both Ariel's birthday and middle school graduation, I knew that there was nothing I could do to make that up. Actually my own dad did better than that—he was home more—and I know in my heart of hearts that if I'm not home at least for the important things that my kids—and my wife—will remember that forever."

When equity and equality are at odds, peers are more likely to opt for equality, and hence for inefficiency. But ultimately, this is a question of *results*. What can we say, in contrast, about *reasons?*

Adult Intimacy

Perhaps the biggest difference between traditional and peer parents is that traditional mothers put their children ahead of their husbands. Peers refuse to prioritize their children above each other because they do not want to sacrifice adult intimacy.

Peer men want to be involved with their children from the beginning, but they want the children to be part of the marriage rather than the only point of the marriage. They do not want to lose their wives to their children.

Some of this determination can come from past experience. Men who have been edged out of the picture in a previous marriage try not to let it happen again. Men and women who had unequal marriages understand more intimately the threats posed by children.

Victor and Tina both had previous brief marriages before they met. When they married and began to discuss having a family, they had definite ideas about what that would require from each of them. Tina had never even considered having children in her first marriage because of what she perceived as the bad mix of her professional and her home life. She was already well on her way to a career as a social service administrator, and her ex-husband was not the kind of person who helped her with any part of her life. She knew she "could barely manage home and work without kids, and when I thought of the demands a career would make and then add what kids would require—there is no way I could do it in my first marriage. Truthfully,

I was scared that I would have to sacrifice one or the other, so I never even seriously thought about it while we were together."

Victor wanted children, but his first marriage had not lasted long. It had foundered under the pressure of finishing his doctoral dissertation and searching for an academic job in a tight job market. When he finally found a teaching job in the Midwest, his wife, passionately attached to her parents and friends in the East, refused to go. Victor went, and they broke up.

By the time Victor and Tine met, they were in their late twenties and each felt that time was running out and that children had to be high on their agenda. As soon as the relationship got serious, discussions about children began, and Tina made it clear that she expected equal participation; Victor was excited about the prospect. After they married, they had plans about how they would time having children so that each person would take a break from work and the other could concentrate on career needs. But then Tina became pregnant four months after their marriage, long before they wanted to start their family.

When the baby came, Tina, who had been so adamant about not being a single mother, fell in love with the baby; she did not give him to Victor as much as he had expected and did not seem to want to talk or make love as much. Victor tried to be sensitive at first, but after some months of this he got mad, "I respect the miracle of birth and all that, but somewhere around the third month, I noticed that neither of us was being very tender with one another. I asked her why, and she looked sort of surprised and said she hadn't really realized she had stopped. So we talked about how the baby was getting that part of her. I wasn't jealous in the classic Freudian sense, but I didn't want that part of our relationship to disappear." This conversation helped Tina get some perspective. She had not dealt with the unanticipated emotional conflicts she was experiencing including her own feelings of neglect by Victor.

After sharing feelings, they recommitted to directing more attention toward one another. They made small, practical changes—for example: Tina started taking the baby in bed with them rather than disapearing into the baby's room, Tina also prepared a two a.m. bottle of her milk so that Victor could help feed the baby before Tina gave up breast-feeding. Both began to feel happy about nurturing this baby together. When Tina returned to work, she was not quite ready to be back but felt better knowing that Victor was with the baby in the mornings and the baby was never in baby care more than five hours a day.

Peer parenting is stabilized and encouraged by peer intimacy. If the parents remain intimate, everyone benefits. Tina continued, "When I got back to work, everyone was commiserating with me for having to come back and leave my baby, and I felt guilty because I was actually pretty happy to be back. I missed my child, but I also missed Vic and I also missed my work. I think the reason I wasn't like all these other women, with their incredible longing for their children, is that I had the distinct feeling that these women were so devoted to their kids not just because they loved their kids but because they were missing something from their husbands." Tina had multiple sources of emotional support, as did the baby and Victor.

Under a traditional division of labor, it is easy for women to be absorbed by their children. Young children offer an uncomplicated destination for limitless affection. But peer couples believe that love for children has to be tempered with love and protection for each other. These men want more than equal standing to their children; they want an adult partnership. Many have been in other marriages in which the spouse was not truly the top priority, and family strength withered as the relationship diminished. Both men and women in this study almost always mentioned, without prompting, how their intimacy, their strong sense of interdependence and friendship, was the foundation they built everything else on. They talked about protecting their relationship by giving it time and thought. They rarely confused family time and adult intimacy. They were usually aware when family responsibilities overwhelmed couple needs and when everything else had to be put on hold so that any necessary emotional repairs could be made.

Discovering the Male Desire to Nurture

Virtually all peer husbands want to father. They love children, and they want to activate and nurture their capacity for tenderness and caretaking.

Sometimes wanting to father is a surprise to the man. Kazuo was brought up in a first-generation Japanese-American household. His father and grandfather were authoritarian, and he knew no other model of parenting. He did not expect to be very involved in his children's lives and in fact was not too keen initially about having children. But he married Marissa, who came from a big, close Italian family and definitely wanted at least two children. Marissa loved family in general and often Kazuo's rather tidy, controlled household was having unannounced visits from multiple relatives from both the United States and Italy. It was not unusual to have a nephew or a niece come visit and stay indefinitely. Kazuo, who felt very put upon in the beginning, came to like it. Then one year, Marissa's sister's drinking problem got completely out of hand, and Marissa suggested they keep her sister's child until the sister successfully rehabilitated. The child stayed with them most of the first several years of her life, and by the time she left, Kazuo was very attached to her and anxious to have children of his own. It was a critical experience: "I got used to being important for Stella. I know I made a difference in this child's life. I feel we saved her, and I wanted to make that kind of difference in my own child's life, but I didn't want to do it the way my father did, like a distant deity. I want to be more like my mother, whom we all adored because we knew how much she adored us. So I come home as early as possible, and I work at home [part time]. I refused a job that would have required weekends. There is no precedent for this in my family, but I have broken other traditions. I married non-Japanese. I never imagined I would do these things. But I have a happy life."

It is easy to see why tender feelings might have traditionally been discouraged in men. Men have always been asked to do the hard thing: go to battle, fight for economic survival, protect the family from enemies and natural disaster. Too soft a nature might get in the way of these hard decisions and acts. On the other hand, we can assume that a significant ability to love passionately and protect is also hardwired into the male animal. From an evolutionary perspective, it stands to reason that we would have strong tendencies to want to love the small and defenseless of our group; otherwise, our helpless but demanding and sometimes annoying children would not evoke the responses necessary to compel adult males to aid their survival.

Peer fathers report two big rewards of coparenting. First, they receive an enormous amount of pleasure from increased intimacy with their child. They are every bit as awed by and bonded to their children as are their wives, and they are pleased to find these capabilities within themselves. Many nonpeer men are frustrated by their inability to connect with their children. They do not want to be so inarticulate that their child does not know how they feel, or vice versa. The small sample for this book might suggest that men with superior interactional abilities are drawn to parenting because they already have emotional skills they merely want to deepen, but it is also clear that some men had the goal first and developed the tools later. One previously married peer father said, "I think I became a parent day by day. In my first marriage, I just turned the whole thing over. I just filled in the time how I felt like it or how I was asked to do it. I never took responsibility. This time, maybe it's just being a father in your forties instead of your twenties, but I don't play second fiddle. I am very much involved in everything. I want to know what they are thinking. I learn from these kids every day. I have that casual time with them—when you're just driving along and you hear what you need to hear."

Second, peer fathers' paternal commitment creates more capacity for intimacy and therefore profits the adult relationship. Peer wives feel their husbands are more emotionally open and less emotionally defensive than other men. Sometimes seeing what a man or woman can offer a child gives a couple an idea of what they can ask from each other.

Pitfalls of Peer Parenting

Peer parenting was new for most of the couples interviewed for this book; only five of the spouses had had parents who could also be called peers. Almost everybody was, in the words of one peer wife, "making it up as we went along." There were plenty of surprises that threatened to put the whole concept in jeopardy.

The Siren Call of Motherhood

In attempting to rearrange the traditional structure of child rearing, peer couples find themselves not only experiencing a different way of loving each other and their children but also confronting some of their own prior beliefs and many of the enduring beliefs of their culture. Joyce and Erik, a couple who showed every sign of being able to resist conventional wisdom about the meaning of motherhood, almost gave in to Joyce's intense attachment to her new baby. Joyce is a twenty-five-year-old nurse living in a town known for its countercultural lifestyles, and she and Erik felt certain that they were going to share all child-rearing responsibilities equally. They had a meticulous plan designed, beginning with Erik's loyal participation in natural child-birth classes. Erik had a carpentry business and could control his hours. They expected no problems.

What was wholly unanticipated was Joyce's feelings surrounding the birth: "I was twenty-three at the time, and you know how sure you are about everything at twenty-three. But right during the birth, I got my first whiff that I wasn't as freed up as I thought I was. [During labor], he was doing what we practiced [in birth class] and I was thinking, 'You macho son of a bitch. Stop telling me what to do.' I knew I was being unreasonable, because we were very strong about calling this *our* pregnancy and *our* labor, but in the nitty-gritty, it was *my* pain, and I resented him telling me what to do like he was really doing the work."

This reaction subsided after the birth but only temporarily: "It didn't get better when we brought the baby home. We had decided to breast-feed, just to get the baby the immunities she needed, and then we were going to go to bottle feeding and I was going to go back to work. First of all, I wanted to breast-feed longer than we agreed to. And Erik was pushing me to give it up because I was hogging the baby all the time, because she was [eating all the time]. And I re-sented that because it was special and my time."

A major confrontation restored the couple to their original concep-tion. Joyce went on, "One night I wanted to hold the baby, and I took her away from him, and Erik just broke down and cried. Now you can tell this is not the kind of guy who cries. . . . But he was crying and saying, 'You're ruining my life' and 'You're ruining our marriage.' I was shocked because I could see how miserable he was, and I saw how I was cutting him out of the family and all of his expectations, which I guess I hadn't taken as seriously as my expectations. It wasn't an overnight switch, but I went back to the original plan."

There has to be something extremely important at stake for the mother of a newborn baby to share mothering. Parenting is a privilege as well as a duty, and only a powerful alternative can be competitive. The physical realities of pregnancy and birth lead almost inexorably to the mother's presumption of senior parent status. It is a long-standing sacred assumption: A woman has the primary rights to her child. Con-servatives and radical feminists alike will support this proposition, and to question it is to risk being attacked from both ends of the political spectrum. This makes it very hard to keep to an egalitarian plan.

It is one thing to yearn for an involved father and quite another to acknowledge that the father has the same rights and access as the mother. This last step, when ideology gets translated to practice, is a radical departure from traditional values and everyday life. Men who ask for equality with mothers have a hard time finding support.

Without support and in the face of a great deal of criticism, it is very hard for coparents to continue. Elsa, a young woman who helps prepare food in a restaurant, said that all she got was criticism for her ideas on shared parenting: "All my girlfriends told me that I'd be sorry, that I'd regret it. They told me that first of all he wouldn't really know as much as me or be as good a dad as I was a mom and that if he was, that would even be worse because if we ever separated, he would try to go for the kids and then where would I be?"

The siren call of motherhood is hard to resist. Many near-peer couples were stopped at this border. Many women would rather raise their children by themselves in an inegalitarian, emotionally disappointing relationship than encourage equal paternal participation with children. Women who want to increase the likelihood of an emotionally fulfilling and collaborative relationship *have* to think about how to share children from the beginning. The lesson of the peers in this book bears repeating: The value *to the child* of having intimate coparents is immeasurable. Overcoming the siren call of motherhood allows a threesome to replace the traditional two-plus-one of mother-child and father.

The Special Case of Stepparenting

Approximately one-third of all marriages are remarriages, and many couples attempting a peer relationship come to a new marriage with children. There is a sparse literature on the impact of these children on marriage, but most of it shows them to complicate the new marriage emotionally and perhaps destabilize it.[6] The irony is that while a failed traditional marriage makes peer marriage newly attractive, stepchildren make it harder to achieve. Stepchildren often create a conflict of interest because they require extensive economic, emotional, and time commitments from the nonbiological parent. The equality of contribution that works well as a concept when both parents are equally invested in the children is less likely and perhaps less desired in these circumstances. This often forces peer parents to go to an equity principle rather than equality.

Everything about stepparenting makes it hard to incorporate the stepchild. Children who live in two different households often resist one of them; if they have a good relationship with their custodial parent, they are likely to see their stepparent's efforts as illegitimate. Being cooperative or loving in the new home may feel disloyal. The more a stepparent looks like a coparent, the more likely it is that the child will feel that the absent biological parent's territory is being violated. Blending two families requires great emotional maturity of everyone concerned, but the likelihood of consistently taking the high road is low.[7]

Research indicates that stepparenting is easier for men than for women. Perhaps this is because less is expected of men, and they have lower standards for themselves about how much participation is required. They do not find the role as overwhelming and threatening as women do. But in peer marriages, both the husband and wife are supposed to be involved, and this makes it hard to follow the most common solution of stepparenting: leaving the parenting duties for the biological parent.

Even when coparenting is the standard, however, there will be greater investment and time spent by the biological parent. No one expects otherwise. Yet it redefines how the household is run and what it means for each adult in the household to have equitable control over the family life-style. About half of the couples who had stepchildren treated them as the responsibility of the biological parent; the others accepted them as a mutual responsibility. Clearly, the latter made the couple more interdependent and the biological parent more grateful, while providing a powerful emotional bond. But stepparenting can compromise time spent with the couple's own children or with each other, and this can cause some conflict. Robin is a young stepmother: "I think it's the hardest thing we do. In all honesty, I didn't want to parent anybody's children but my own. But I was forced to see that if I didn't pitch in, it would ruin our relationship. He had too much on his shoulders, and I had to be part of the solution. I guess I had always been happy to do what I signed up for, and this was something I hadn't signed up for but I had to do anyhow. This has required more maturity of me than I think I had at the beginning, but it's working well now."

This was the subject that elicited the most war stories from peer couples. Two peer married couples had bitter fights about stepparenting; almost all of them found it difficult for a long time. One husband said, "Basically we went through about ten years of hell on this, and I don't even know how we got through it." A wife in her fifties still smarts over what she feels was a real lapse in an otherwise fair relationship. She remembers children who never cooperated in the house, paying for outrageous telephone bills that stressed their budget, never knowing when their household would be disrupted by some crisis, and feeling impotent about influencing their conduct. Step-parenting sorely tested the ideals of teamwork, joint purpose, and egalitarian contribution. Many people were ultimately able to say, like this peer mother, "Finally, I think they accept me as part of their family," but in general, the high standards of participation that peer couples expect of each other make stepparenting one of the most difficult trials of peer relationships.

The Private (and Exclusionary) Mother's Club

Another major and, in this case, universal hurdle to equality in child rearing is the integration of men into the closely held worlds of women—the playgroups, swimming lessons, and school committees that bring mothers together. They are the instant coffee dates, arranged as suddenly as pickup basketball games, when people find themselves with a little time between dropping off children and their next appointment. The world of mothers exists in all the locations associated with early and middle child raising; they can be organized settings, like a PTA meeting, or environments that generally collect mothers, like a pediatric office. The locations vary, but the distinguishing characteristic does not: These are female environments. If a man is present, he is immediately understood to be temporarily substituting for the real member. Depending on the place, he may be graciously engaged as a welcome visitor or resented as an interloper.

These environments are as foreign to most men as hunting clubs are to most women. When a husband first appears with his infant at the pediatrician's office for a well-baby check-up or as the parent who volunteers to take the preschool group on an outing, he is likely to feel awkward. Those who interact with him are likely to be equally artless. Harold described taking one of his sons to a physician after the boy hurt his knee: "This doctor did not want to deal with me as the responsible parent. I was the delivery man who brought Devon in. He wanted so badly to be talking to Devon's mother. He kept saying things like, 'Tell your wife to give him this pill at this time,' or 'I'm sure your wife will want to change these bandages at least once a day.' I lost patience with him, and I can't remember exactly what I said, but I let him have it. I was the parent here and not my wife, and to stop acting like I wasn't there. It was incredibly frustrating."

It is frustrating to be subtly or even not so subtly told that it is illegitimate for men to take on a primary parental role. It is unsettling to have no natural allies. Even if the mothers are not hostile or bemused, they rarely think to include fathers in their collective routines. Harold had to force his way in: "I felt like I was in sixth grade again and no one would let me in the 'in' group. I could see that all these women were setting up afternoon school activities and exchanging choice information, like who is the best swimming teacher, and making it easier for their kids to be friends. No one was including Devon because no one felt comfortable about getting to know *me*. I made a special effort to engage two of the women in conversation, and I had Rena [his wife] call and get me into some of the programs so I could meet these other mothers on an informal basis. I think it took me a year longer than it should have for me to make friends and for people to think of calling me to see if I was available."

These informal networks of mothers not only treat men as aliens but are organized on the premise that every child will have a dominant parent. Consequently, the parenting culture is ill matched to a couple who shares child raising equally. A twenty-eight-year-old peer mother said, "I'm not always the one who is there in the mornings, so I miss some of the instructions and I miss things like the time Karen was the only child who didn't bring something beginning with *S* to class because everyone assumed I'd know even though it was Jeff who picked her up and dropped her off that day, and they didn't give him the slip with the instructions on it. And I can just see them get chummier and chummier over the school year but not with me because I'm not there every day."

More daunting, most traditional parents believe they are raising their families the right way, and they can be unpleasantly judgmental about parenting strategies that depart from their own. Most peer couples are resilient—they have had to be independent and secure in their philosophy to get this far—but nonetheless need approval and encouragement. Peer fathers get a lot of compliments, but they are aware that most other men have ambivalent or contemptuous feelings about their dedication to parenting. Peer mothers know that more traditional mothers do not believe in the peer approach to parenting. So peer couples often turn inward and make the family their social group or look for environments where they might find other couples with the same parenting philosophy. Some couples mentioned that they sought out neighborhoods to live in that had a high concentration of working couples, hoping to have a better chance of finding people like themselves. A lack of a ready peer group causes them some headaches, but it doesn't seem to be enough to force a return to a more traditional pattern.

The Difficulty of Coming to Agreement

One of the positive aspects of a traditional division of labor is that when two partners vociferously disagree, the person with the job can end the argument by pulling rank. This may not always be the best solution for the child—child raising isn't so easy that one person can always be right—but it keeps peace in the house if one person is supposed to back down before the other.

In peer marriage, there is no resorting to the standard parenting formula of male discipline and female nurturance. It is against the credo of egalitarian families to use some of those utilitarian dodges like, "Wait until your father gets home." There is no support for systematically delegating the hard parts of parenting or making one parent "the bad guy." These divisions may happen because of natural personality differences; but even then, the equity-equality mix means that eventually each person has to do the jobs he or she would rather not.

The good news here is that no one parent is blamed with the outcomes of parenting. Gone is the concept of maternal blame for how children turn out. Gone are the days of theorizing that gay children result from domineering mothers or autistic children from cold mothers. The sharing of responsibility is important because synchronizing a joint child-raising approach is hard. Unless couples happen to view discipline in the same way, they have to negotiate or fight about how to proceed. Since no one has more authority, there must be reconciliation of any major disagreement in discipline or approach. The children often keep the parents honest in this respect, as one woman noted: "Oh you know kids. They are always looking for a hole in your defenses, and if you give them even a little, tiny opening, well, they're in it and gone. When we argue about how to handle something—and we do, we do— then the kids are right up there trying to stop a common conclusion— you know, divide and conquer. I suppose this happens to all parents, but I think they know that I can't just step aside."

Traditional father and mother roles can look attractive after this kind of battling over philosophical territory. Children, too, learn the traditional parenting roles from television and friends. If parents start to look like the classic expressive mom and the disciplinarian dad, the children will start reinforcing those identities by the way they relate to each parent, and the couple's hopes for coparenting begin to un- ravel. Children go through periods when, for many reasons, they are more attracted to one or the other parent. A parent will feel troubled when a child plays type against type. Redirecting the child's focus (for example, the child's quicker turn to mom for hugs and kisses) is hard. Inserting dad when mom is requested flies in the face of what seems to be the child's needs, and all loving parents want their child's needs to be met. But sometimes, if the parent pushes through, a new role can fit comfortably for both the parent and the child. As one father said, "Who wants to be where they're not wanted? I hated going swimming [when the child preferred his mother to be there], but finally Bobbie let me know he was glad I was there."

Given pressures from the outside, it is especially distressing when the couple themselves cannot come to agreement about child raising. Charles and Melanie went through the worst years of their marriage when their son was young and they had great differences about how to react. When Zachary defied Melanie, she would immediately pun- ish him. Melanie felt Charles was ridiculously permissive and feared that Charles was going to create a spoiled child. They fought so much about this difference in discipline that both began to worry that their child was more in danger from their two different and opposed styles of child rearing than he was from his own misdeeds.

The troubles were accentuated because both were self-confident, involved parents and each was convinced the other person was the dangerous one. The differences between them were taking their toll on their friendship. At the time of the interview, they had made an appointment with a couselor and agreed to follow whatever course of action she recommended. Peer couples see that a lack of teamwork can be ominous for the peer relationships, and parenting difficulties have to be resolved as soon as possible.

The Desire To Be Equally—or More—Loved

Another related peer parenting dilemma, perhaps not surprisingly, is jealousy. A traditional husband does not expect his children to go to him as much as they seek his wife, at least when the children are young. But a peer husband does not want to be second choice. And women who have usually been able to take their children's preference for granted now have formidable competition. Although every peer mother truly loves having a peer father for a husband, quite a few, when asked if they ever feel uneasy about the degree of their children's attachment to their father, said, "Of course." A thirty-eight-year-old banker married to her childhood sweetheart, who was a youth worker with the police department, said, "Well, I have a little problem because he is really the nurturing one between us. I'm good too, but Rog is always available, always calm, has great ideas in a crisis. Throughout college and in graduate school, he was the parent of choice.... They call him much more than they call me. And even though I know they love me, I wouldn't be telling the truth if I didn't tell you it bothers me some of the time."

Mothers in the United States may be the popular scapegoat for child-related problems, but they are also used to getting their share of glorification. Just as women learn to want and expect compliments about their appearance, so they expect to get points for parenthood. Sharing those points is not easy. Not getting special recognition can hurt and even feel like criticism. Even if peer mothers are perfectly happy that their husband gets his due rewards from the children and others, several wanted to feel just a "little more special."

Restructuring Work

Not all impediments to peer marriage are psychological. The workplace could care less about helping out peer parents, and many subtle differences in the structure of men's versus women's work force participation make it hard to coparent.

One of the problems for most men and women is that men are supposed to take "men's jobs" and women are likely to be channeled into "women's jobs." Women are more likely to be employed in the service sector and in lower-paying jobs where working reduced hours is easier. Jobs like substitute teacher, waitress, market research interviewer, or temporary secretary offer flexibility—but at a price. Women pick or resign themselves to these kinds of jobs because they combine well with child raising, but that is a double-edged sword: jobs that allow the flexibility tend to pay less, have more of a salary ceiling, and provide less interest and engagement. This differentation can be found even within professions: Paralegals are more often women; full-time lawyers are much more often men.

When medical emergencies happen, or teacher-parent conferences are scheduled at 11 A.M., the parent with the "woman's job" is expected to go. This determination is based on a rational assessment of how to protect the bigger income source and of the likelihood that the "woman's job" can be replaced more easily if the woman gets in trouble for taking care of the family during working hours. Over time, this division of jobs makes it impossible for equal child-care contribution. The woman becomes the primary caretaker because it is the only plan that makes economic sense.

Near peers tell story after story about this kind of situation: "She was a school teacher; she could get away by midafternoon, so it just got so she was the one who would do everything." "She earned about 10 percent what I did. If I took off in the middle of the day, I could kiss this job good-bye, so we relied on her." "I'd be happy to take care of the kids if I didn't have to work, but that's just the way it is. We made a conscious decision that she would only work part time so that she could be available when the kids needed her." Overall, it was clear, the structure of work made it hard to avoid a division of labor on parenting.

Yet this chapter shows many couples who were able to restructure work so that it supported their parenting goals. It is almost never automatic, but they make it happen. Victor and Tina again serve as an example. They have two children, one nine and one five years old. They planned to collaborate on child raising from the beginning, and they do. On a typical morning, Victor gets up about a half-hour before Tina. He showers and shaves before the first child begins to stir. A smallish, personally fastidious man of thirty-seven, he is usually dressed by seven and has his morning in order when five-year-old

Lisa, still half asleep, crawls in bed with her mother and starts pulling at her to get up. This is Victor's cue to make sure that their son, Max, is getting himself ready to get to school on time. It has been Victor's responsibility more or less since the children were born to see to it that they get up and are dressed and fed in the morning. He enjoys the ritual of making breakfast, and he likes giving his wife a little extra sleep because he knows how much she appreciates it.

Things have not always worked this smoothly. Tina got pregnant while Victor was a new assistant professor in a large research university. At the same time that his colleagues congratulated him on the coming baby, their jokes let him know that they thought it was a foolhardy step to take so early in his career.

After the baby came, Victor quickly learned that his commitment to coparenting was deeply threatening to some of his colleagues. He did not get critiqued for joining a Lamaze birth class, but he did get teased about wanting to talk about it. "I guess talking about baby topics to colleagues is in bad taste. I'm not stupid. I stopped talking about it."

After Max was born, life became much more complicated. Victor took his turn caring for the baby during the night and during the day. Tina breast-fed during the first six weeks, but she found it impossible once she went back to work at her agency. Moreover, she derived great pleasure from Victor's enthusiasm and joy in feeding the baby, so she was happy to switch to bottle feeding. Then they decided to take turns bringing their seven-month-old son to work with them.

Tina was stunned by her coworkers' reactions: "All these women who oo-ed and ah-ed over the baby pictures were gagging at the idea of my baby crying in my office. The ones under me weren't bad; my secretary seriously thought about bringing her one-year-old, and she and I had this fantasy about putting a darn good nursery together. But the department heads and visitors from other parts of the agency were offensive. They didn't say anything to me directly, but they obviously didn't like it, and I would hear gossip about what a pain in the ass I was with my kid."

It was worse for Victor. His first trip to the university with Max was treated by his colleagues as great show and tell. And when he spent the entire afternoon with the child in his office, they assumed that some unexpected work had arisen that prevented Victor from taking the baby back home to Tina once everyone had had a chance to see him. "None of them put two and two together. They knew Tina had gone back to work, and they knew we couldn't afford quality child care. I wasn't going to put him in some awful infant care. What did they think the baby is supposed to do—take care of himself?"

But the people in his department soon figured it out when Victor stopped joining them for lunch, and they began to hear Max in his office. Victor started to hear negative gossip, which infuriated him: "Basically, they implied that I was not serious about my work. It got so I would sneak him in in the morning and sneak him out if I could. It was insane. You'd think it would be better on a college campus, wouldn't you? The absolute low point was when someone, I think in a supportive way—but I'm not sure—pasted this Gary Trudeau cartoon on my door that shows this father telling his boss that he is going to set up a computer at home so he can see more of his kid, and the boss starts laughing and calling the guy 'house wimp.' Well, I saw this cartoon on my door and I tore it off, not sure of what it meant, but not wanting to give words to what I thought some of my colleagues, and maybe even some of the students, were thinking."

Victor's colleagues feared that Victor's commitment to active child rearing would undermine his productivity, and, in fact, it did. He could no longer make as much headway in writing his book during the day or the evenings on his child-care shift. He traveled less to professional conferences. Tina also encountered impediments to her own career advancement. She had to decline a much higher paying job because it required regular travel around the state.

The couple was exhausted. They started using more child care but found themselves financially strapped. Those were hard years according to Tina but also "some of our closest moments." Although they were stressed and, according to Tina, "Our sex life went to hell," she said, "I can't tell you how good it was to have each other and hold these kids together and bring them up as a pair." It was clear to both of them, however, that if Victor did not invest more time in his writing, he would be denied tenure. Consequently, they borrowed money to make changes in their living arrangement that would lighten their child-care burden. They renovated the basement of their tiny house to create an additional bedroom and bathroom where a student could live in exchange for child care, and they eventually patched together a complicated child-care system.

The financial pressures alone impressed on them the irrationality of having another child, but they wanted three children and feared that if they waited, the spacing between the children would be too wide to allow them ever to be easy companions. So Tina became pregnant with Lisa, and as soon as the pregnancy became obvious, she began hearing even greater skepticism over the seriousness of her career commitment and dire predictions for her work performance.

Victor's tenure decision was imminent. He tried to conceal his wife's pregnancy until after the lengthy evaluation process, but several of his colleagues found out, and soon everyone knew. Victor had been working long hours in his off-parent moments, and his efficiency was greatly enhanced when he and Tina started hiring child care. Because he finished his book and because his scholarly writings were well accepted in his field, Victor was granted tenure and promoted. He and Tina felt that for six years they had carried a weight so heavy that they had not dared to notice how crushing it had become.

After tenure, Victor's public stance on child rearing changed dramatically and he began to proselytize about the joys of fatherhood. "I'd say things like, 'What if you dropped dead tommorrow? Would your kids even know you?' I had lots of fun—especially since you could see they knew I was right and they really didn't want to deal with it."

Practical Solutions

A good deal of peer parenting comes down to simple pragmatics. Peer couples anxious to enable others with similar ambitions mentioned a number of solutions.

Choose Your Work Carefully

Some jobs are better than others for raising children. The first step to peer parenting is figuring out what will work. One man who had always dreamed of being a television reporter realized it was too inflexible, too consuming, and too arbitrary to readily allow for peer parenting. Many men and women backed away from big law firms, corporate business, jobs that required extensive travel, jobs that wanted the husband and wife to look and act traditional. Picking the right job from the beginning was best, but most men and women found themselves making adjustments as they went along.

The Timing of Parenthood

Pregnancy is not always controllable, but for the most part, couples who had their children after they had decided that they wanted to coparent did better than couples in an ongoing situation that had to be modified. Bargaining first seemed to keep most spouses honest; changing the rules later usually required much more artful negotiations.

Timing was also important in terms of not scuttling the wife's work pattern too early in her career. Whether it was a high-status, high-paying job, or a lower-status job that had more turnover, having a track record somewhere before asking for special terms of employment for child raising worked better. Couples who were older and more secure in their philosophy, and with a little more money, had an easier time of putting together a peer parenting plan that worked.

If Necessary, Use the Alternating Model

Sometimes it is impossible for both people to parent at once. There are periods in certain careers—a medical residency, the first years in a law firm or professorship, an employee management program—when too much attention to child care would mean the end of the career. Some couples were able to make bargains of alternating responsibility. One man who was a doctor promised, and delivered on his pledge, that if his wife cared for the children through his residency, he would take a sabbatical while she went back to get her graduate degree in nursing. A young woman took care of her children during her theological training, but her husband took an extended leave of absence from his job to be the primary parent when she took her first job as a clergywoman. Several older couples who had been quite traditional in their past turned the terms of their marriage around. The husband retired or took over household duties and became more invested in the children while the woman spread her wings, went back to work, or simply got her turn at driving their life-style.

Symbolic Lapses Are Important

Small things matter. It really does matter who picks up the socks, or if everyone does their fair share of laundry, or shopping for daily needs. Making exceptions to tasks is dangerous—and part of the slippery slope that cost many near peers their dream of being a closer partnership. Vic and Tina related one incident that she believed was a turning point in their commitment to being peer parents: "He and I had agreed to take Max and his three best friends on a weekend camping trip for his birthday. The date was set, and Max was expecting it. He'd been excited about it for weeks. And then Victor gets told the the faculty retreat has been changed to this weekend, and it's very important that he be there. Now you have to remember that this is before tenure, and so Victor comes home and his first instinct is, well, of course, we have to change the camping weekend, or that I should take the boys alone. We had a very serious talk. I explained that I was willing to do this but that this was the beginning of considering me and the children flexible and therefore secondary and his commitments to the job first. We both decided that he had right on his side—that it was his department's problem if they cancel something at the last moment and then try to make everyone change their plans. So Victor went back and simply said he couldn't and that it was a family promise and he couldn't do that to his family. I don't think it was a big hit, but it was great to be able to figure that out together and stick with it."

Many couples did make compromises to keep their work or get promoted. But it was also true that couples mentioned many incidents of solidarity when the couple and the family's right to be the center of life was affirmed, even if it was inconvenient or risky to do so.

Be Patient

Many couples counseled patience. They talked about the difficulty of equality compared to equity and that they had to keep working at giving each other a fair deal that did not turn into the old deal. They felt that a lot of leeway had to be given to both partners because the familiar ways would sneak back in and the important thing was to avoid treating each slipup as a question of bad faith. Both men and women said it took time for men to feel that a commitment to parenting was natural and easy and time for women to give up some control and enjoy a team effort.

Get Help

The use of hired or family child care help was strongly advised. Even committed parents need a break. When both partners work outside the home, there is a tendency to use all spare time as family time, but relationships that want to maintain a deep friendship need time alone. Peer marriages—most marriages, in fact—work best when the couple's love affair is protected. Coparenting, the most original part of peer marriage, cannot be allowed to swamp the relationship.

Keep Accounts

One peer wife said, "There has to be a little accounting system in the back of your head to make sure you just haven't backed right into being your mom and dad." Nobody wanted an exact exchange, but they cautioned that it was too easy for the woman to find herself doing more than a fair share, mostly because she could do it better or because she liked to do it more. No one wanted to mandate rigid job sharing that kept people from favored tasks and special talents, but many cautioned about letting things slide so that women ended up taking over parenting. As time went on and couples worked out a system, there were definitely relaxations of earlier, more rigid dispensation of duties. But couples warned that too generous an interpretation of coparenting usually resulted in mothers' taking over all the details of children's social and school life, which started to make them into primary parents again. Benign vigilance was necessary—not from distrust but as a counterweight to the pull of tradition. Most suggest some kind of measurement scheme so that couples know when they have ceased to meet their own expectations.

Conclusions: Coparenting as a Reinstitutionalization of Marriage

Earlier we discussed the willingness of distant fathers to leave marriages. Is coparenting a potential cure to the divorce revolution? Certainly it is hard for peer fathers to leave their marriage, and it is extremely hard for a mother to want to let that kind of father go. There are many ties—emotional, sexual, financial—that help a marriage through hard times. We have seen that the mere fact of having children does not, by itself, have the necessary weight. The majority of divorces have young children in them. Something beyond biological relationship is needed to keep fathers attached to their families. It has to be the attachment of love and mutual need. A father has to feel that if he leaves, his children will be more than materially disadvantaged; they will be emotionally bereft. Father and child will lose something elemental from their daily lives. The father, like the mother, must know that no one else can take his place.

Moreover, his placement at the center of family life makes it hard for his wife to leave the relationship. Most women feel deeply obligated to give their children a good life. When a marriage has problems or gets boring or in some other way does not meet today's high expectations of personal fulfillment, women as well as men yearn for greener pastures. When a man is a coparent, his stock is worth more, and the idea of taking children away from an excellent father is extremely wrenching. Coparenting is not by itself an irrefutable defense against divorce, but it cannot help but make a divorce less attractive. It is impossible to predict the long-term viability of all the couples in this book, but they seem particularly happy and stable.

Might fathers run away from their children anyway? Do they just get overwhelmed such that no amount of coparenting would keep them embroiled in the family drama? Most mothers, and many fathers, will tell anyone who will listen that raising a child is the hardest thing they have ever done. Even the most committed of parents share many feelings of deep disappointment, anger at being misled or mistreated, rage at insubordination, pain from lack of appreciation, or general feelings of inadequacy in response to the child's needs. Still, mothers rarely desert their children, and they have traditionally taken the full brunt of these unhappier parts of parenting. One supposes they bear them because they find the rewards extraordinary. Is there any reason to doubt that if men get the same amount of compensating pleasure from their children, more of them will want to stick around? Perhaps the men in these peer couples are extremely rare, self-selected, children-loving people who are so atypical of other men that the lessons of their relationships are too unusual to extrapolate to other husbands and wives. Still, it seems possible that if fathering were more intense, fathers would be more committed to their families. They should also be more committed to their partner; it only makes sense. Sharing the stress and the triumphs of child raising creates an extraordinary bond, whereas carrying the brunt of difficult or frightening experiences alone creates alienation and undermines solidarity.

The great potential for peer parenting is this: By giving the child two parents, the couple gets more marriage. What may seem at first like a disinvestment in the children pays dividends in love and understanding. Not all parents can manage to put parenting back into paternity, but for those who do, the effect on the relationship and on the children is profound. Can it be done on a large scale? There are signs that our collective antipathy toward the fully committed father is mitigating. Busy women are grateful to have a husband to share the work and lessen the guilt. A double income allows each person to earn less than they would have to earn if they were the only earner. Expectations of men and criteria for a good husband are changing. Businesses are looking at the costs that divorce exacts on the workforce and more are deciding that being "family friendly"—and giving parents some support—are in the long-term interest of the company.

The peer couples described in this book are in the vanguard of parenthood. They know they are going against expectation, but they are courageous in their determination to bend the social structure to their will. Almost none of them have found coparenting a natural fit; all have had to modify their ideals at one point or another. But over time, they have created a model for friends, family, and acquaintances to watch and wonder about. What may have begun as an ideological commitment, a child-raising philosophy, or just a desire for a fair deal has become much more than that: the reinstitutionalization of marriage itself.

— *Chapter 6* —

The Future
of Peer Marriage

P eer marriage is becoming more widely practiced. I believe that many peer couples are a model most of their children will wish to emulate. But it will not take generations before peer marriages become common. More women are in the workplace and want and need a real helpmate. Although these trends have not produced a tidal wave of male support up to this time, there is creeping incrementalism; women are becoming vocal about getting what they need at the same time that men are reassessing what they want.

Peer marriage may be part of a general reassessment of what life is all about. In the past twenty years, women have joined the work force in large numbers, and although there is still a regrettable amount of sexism in hiring, many of these women have been given more responsibility, higher office, more possibility of impressive salary. But all of this asks for time—lots of time—and not a little of one's soul. Ordinary jobs also extract more and more time. The new technology—faxes, car telephones, and modems—make everyone in offices work harder, and the economy makes the average working man and woman hustle harder. Most couples feel that dual income is necessary to maintain a household. And the majority of women also regard work and income as sources of respect and fulfillment. So the questioning is not so much about working but the place of work in personal and family life. The exchange of income for time is now being rethought by both fast trackers and ordinary workers: What is the point of work? Is it supposed to enhance individual glory or couple and family happiness? What is the right mix of individual fulfillment and obligation to the loved ones in one's life? What modifications of work might be necessary so that it doesn't eat up all the quality time available and leave none to secure parental and spousal satisfaction? Women are not asking to give up work but they do not want it to overwhelm their personal life. On the other hand, they want to keep the respect and self-fulfillment the workplace has brought them. Perhaps more revolutionary, more men are also taking a look at the whole picture and questioning whether the traditional roles they have played will bring them what they really want. Men have been affected by the women's movement and by the strong women they meet who want them to share the home and parenting experience. The fragmentation of the family has also been a spur for thought: What is the outcome of not having a father—and a strong relationship—for the future of the family?

Putting ideology and practice together, however, has been difficult. The world of work was not created for this change in male and female relationships, and we are still a generation that has more role models for a traditional relationship that we do for an egalitarian one. Still, today's men and women have developed a taste for partnership, for family, and for each other. Perhaps more than any other time in history, men and women want their spouse to be their friend; they want to be in love, but they also want companionship. Women want respect, fairness, collaboration, and an intense relationship. Many men want to give it to them, but the poor fit between work and relationships has made this difficult. Couples who are giving their all to the work world find themselves depleted with nothing left for home. Overwhelmed men and women start to think that maybe the work world—and especially the fast track—is not an ideal after all.

Some couples have given in to these pressures by becoming more traditional. Well-trained women with high self-esteem stay home for a while to make sure their children are getting enough of them. They forgo ambition or income so that family life can be better. But most of these women do not want to be traditional wives. Their return to the household is not a tacit agreement to return to traditional power differences. These women are upset when traditional male-female differences start to return. They do not want their husband to feel he is entitled to control the relationship. They are disappointed when they do not get enough of him—for themselves or for the children.

This book shows that what women want is not best accomplished by a traditional division of labor. Nor is it easily obtained when both men and women work on a fast track. Most peer couples maintain their relationship goals by folding work into the relationship rather than vice versa. Critical to this process is the conscious—or unconscious—recognition that the relationship cannot be sacrificed to the work demands of a provider role. If this book has found anything at all, it is that allowing the provider role to dominate family organization not only makes it impossible to have quality—it also makes it unlikely to have equity, companionship, paternal investment, and the kind of deeper friendship and respect that women and men say they want. The provider role orients the wife to the husband's needs and the children's needs rather than the husband and wife to each other and then mutually to the family. Over time, husbands expect a certain amount of obedience and get used to modifying their wife's and family's needs according to the demands of their work. The couple, by taking care of different parts of life, become more distant to one another, and there is the danger of both overestimating and underestimating each other. There are failures of realism and a diminution of shared interests when people live in parallel worlds. Men take women's labor for granted or greatly underestimate what their wife's day requires. Women fall into the trap of evaluating the success of their marriage by life-style rather than intimacy.

And these neotraditional women suffer because our culture celebrates intimacy and friendship, and women can't quite give up on the desire to have a truly close psychological connection with their husband. Men, less focused on the need for psychic connection, are nonetheless searching for a satisfying partnership, and they get bored and angry when their marriage is reduced to modest recapitulations of their day, forays into parenting, or wifely recriminations punishing them for their emotional deficits. All partners, peer and traditional, remember their courting days and look nostalgically back on the infatuation, passion, or love. But while peer couples take comfort in the deepening of friendship, those in traditional and near-peer relation-ships cannot help but notice how much intimacy has been lost.

If you ask traditional couples to identify what is really important to them, almost all of them say a partner who is a best friend, a partner who is a good parent, and an intimate and loyal family environment. But when traditional couples predicate family life on the husband's long hours in the work force, allowing minimal overlapping time of family members, it is easy to believe that traditional couples no longer believe in or have lost track of their own values. It is not that the economic part of the contract is unimportant or inappropriately satis-fying. Being secure, even successful and ambitious, are not antithet-ical to peer marriage. But without the addition in each spouse's life of nontrivial collaboration with their partner, the relationship and the family become marginalized. Children are deprived of paternal time; the wife, deprived of paternal teamwork and spousal intimacy; and the partners will not become each other's real best friend. Comparing what people want to what people do, it does not seem unfair to take traditional and near-peer couples to task for saying the noble thing and living the easiest solution to the material dream.

These couples have been seduced by the proximal rewards of in-equality. They have set their sights on financial security or success, which they rationalize will benefit the marriage and the family in the long run. In fairness, they also choose a traditional family structure because they believe that men are better suited to the work force—or at least that women are better suited to raising children and guiding the family. But while no one doubts women's unique biological rela-tionship to children, there is certainly adequate evidence that children need other adults in their lives, not the least of whom is their father. The role of the father has been underplayed by traditional couples because it might require too much modification of the provider role. Moreover, this determined diminishment of the father's role suits the general purposes of the status quo: It relieves each sex of the other sex's responsibilities. It allows specialization along traditions that are familiar and therefore comforting. Women can retreat from a work force that intimidates them or may not be going well. They can concentrate on their previous preparation and desire for motherhood. Men can escape the more mundane chores of household labor. Am-bitious men can concentrate on taking their identity from their work; less ambitious men can prove their worth by slogging through wearing jobs that support their family. They can escape from the unfamiliar territory of everyday parenting.

Still, even resolutely traditional men and women see cracks in the traditional model of marriage when they confront modern divorce statistics. They have to ask themselves, why, if traditional or even near-peer marriages are a good model, they haven't spared the inhabitants from divorce. Would more duty and sacralization of marriage prevent divorce—or would a better marriage? In fact, many of the modern church-based marital movements such as marriage encounter are moving toward a peer model. Some are based on hierarchy, but many of them are basically organized to teach men to listen to women, to teach the couple as a unit how to collaborate, and to refocus the relationship as the center of the couple's life together.

This is not to say that peer marriages are invulnerable—there are no data on the longevity of these kind of relationships—and this sample of marriages cannot test their long-term durability. Still, they seem remarkably solid, and they have constructed many blocks to dissolution. The most formidable is the child-raising team. They have also created a context for conversation and action that includes equal participation and equal decision making. They have two people instead of one taking the role of relationship expert and maintenance person. Men learn expressive skills from parenting and help keep the relationship on track. Men and women, because they are living quite similar lives, need some similar supports, and help is appreciated for what it is: proof of affection and respect. Peer women are much less likely to feel emotionally abandoned by their husband than are traditional wives: the amount of interaction allows them many sources from which to get confirmation of worth and commitment. They have learned, as a couple, to act as advisers for one another, and they can tolerate benign honesty from one another. Their identities are not fused, not dependent, but stronger for the collaboration between them. The considerable time they spend together allows the partners to keep current in each other's lives and thereby be the best friend who does not have to be brought up to date on why something is an issue or what might be the right way to handle a growing dilemma.

Peer couples are notable for their ability to negotiate and their lack of defensive turf building. One of the main outcomes of the modification of the provider role is that children are mutual territory and women are not utterly absorbed by child raising. Children detract less from adult intimacy. Peer husbands feel very different from traditional husbands about the role children play in the couple's emotional life.

Peer spouses constantly have to be on their guard, however, or they fall into the roles they have been prepared for all their lives. These men and women have grown up in the culture that made traditional and near-peer marriages, and the urge to slide into hierarchical slots does not go away easily. Again, the team approach helps maintain mutual responsibility—that and maintaining a wary respect for the power of the provider role to create rank and separate the spouses.

Research on working-, middle- and upper-middle-class black couples shows a much more egalitarian profile.[1] At the same time that poor black families have become greatly disadvantaged by economic deprivation, single motherhood, and a culture of males' leaving the family or maintaining only a loose association with it, intact black families, especially those of the middle class, have derived a certain silver lining from the uncertain connection between black males and stable labor force participation. Because many black couples have a woman whose income is equal to or better than or more stable than the male's, they are more likely to take a cooperative approach to caring for the family. The couple does what it needs to survive and prosper, and men do women's traditional tasks with little feeling of stigma, disinterest, or inappropriateness. There were seven black or mixed black and other race couples interviewed for this book, and they fit this model. In fact, they were less likely to need an ideology, a previous marriage, or an insistent female partner to have a peer marriage. For each of these couples, it was assumed from the beginning that the marriage would be a partnership and that there would be two workers, two participating parents, two household managers.

For couples with no background of parental peer relationships or who have to resist the traditions of a family organized around the provider role, the conversion to a peer philosophy is a lot less natural. Calculating equity and translating it into equality can be too conscious, too awkward as a bookkeeping effort for many couples. When the provider role has been traditional or male job opportunities are tantalizing, it is easy to put equality on hold and try to find some other system of fairness. But pure equity is a dangerous solution.

Some couples can do it for a while. There are couples, who have alternated taking care of the children while the other person went to school or who traveled and gave up their own job prospects temporarily in order to enable the other person to have a wonderful opportunity, but these couples did fulfill their promise to give the sacrificing partner his or her turn when the first goal had been accomplished. Unfortunately, this does not always happen. I can still hear the plaintive and betrayed feeling of one now-peer wife who left her near-peer husband: "I kept waiting for my turn. He told me it would come. And it took me a long time to realize that it was never, ever going to happen." The safest way to create a deep friendship is to keep that fair deal alive, and that means each person must do his or her share for each other's dreams and their mutual responsibilities. Equity is a tantalizing theory, and it makes perfectly good sense, except that when it reinstitutes traditional male and female roles, hierarchy almost inevitably results—and the opportunity for empathy and teamwork is lost. Collaborating on everyday life and experiencing many things, especially children, jointly, is necessary to mutual intimacy. Making sure that no one person is stuck with low-status and uninteresting housework helps maintain the elevation of both partners as equals. It is very hard to get around these effects in any other than a peer formation.

The Costs of Peer Marriage

No solution is without its own drawbacks. And like every other bargain in life, peer marriage has costs. The costs are considerable, and they are one of the reasons some peer marriages devolve into something else or never start to begin with.

Trespassing the Biological Imperative

The most obvious cost may be the fear that one is tinkering with the very nature of male and female abilities and that the family will ultimately suffer. Most peer couples are quite sure of the rightness of their path, but all of them have gone through periods when lack of support made them worry that they were undercutting their futures. Women who work worry that their children are not getting enough of them—and there are plenty of pundits to tell them that they personally are responsible for any problem their child might have. Peer parents have the advantage of adding male parenting, but it is still true that peer mothers, by the very nature of the deal, are not full-time moms.

Endangering the Family's Economic Future

The pressure from changing the nature of the marital bargain can be particularly scary when both partners compromise jobs. In-laws and parents howl in protest; fast-track friends may or may not hold their opinion, but even if they keep quiet, everyone knows it is virtually un-American not to maximize potential success. Some peer couples do not have that problem. Several couples interviewed for this book did not have children (although I consciously kept most childless couples out of the book because I felt that childlessness is not a true test of an egalitarian relationship), and these couples did not generally sacrifice work for the relationship. Couples without children can more easily create a collegial relationship; work is a major part of their teamwork. Still, even couples without children could miss each other, since work seems to expand to fit the time available. In fact, one childless peer couple was busy plotting an early retirement plan so they could open up a business together in the tropics. The childless peer couples in this study had high-paying jobs, and this allowed them to hire others, which allowed them to compromise their work less. Still, there were moments in most of these couples' lives when opportunities were relinquished because of the costs to the couple's commitment to each other.

The average peer couple made income and success sacrifices, and sometimes it hurt to do that. One woman academic was offered a prestigious chair at the place she most wanted to go. Her husband had a hard-to-find and almost irreplaceable job. She had to turn her job offer down—as he, some years before, had turned down the one job in the country he wanted more than the job he had. The pain of those losses never completely goes away. I heard no regrets—just sadness that it could not all fall into place. Still, for some, this cost—and often the attendant level of income that is forgone—is experienced for just what it is, a loss. And some people may not be strong enough in their convictions about their relationship and family to withstand the temptation of a great, and perhaps one-time, opportunity, even if it would scuttle peer status.

Forgoing income is almost a cardinal sin in this country. And while each person has an idea of what he or she would need to feel economically fortunate and happy, it seems almost a maxim that whatever people have, they always want more. Forgone income will come back to haunt many couples, and conflicts or recriminations can occur. If the couple is solid about the goal of the relationship, these arguments can be settled well, but if the family economy has taken a turn for the worse or if personal ambitions are not adequately fulfilled, there is the danger of major regrets and recriminations.

Being a Member of the Equity Police

Another real cost is the accounting that has to take place from time to time to make sure that the couple remains fair and egalitarian. When the relationship is going through a rough patch, this can feel petty and punishing. Getting upset about who took the children to piano lessons last, or who is doing more reading with them, or who is dealing with parental medicare benefits or other projects, can get antagonistic. Equity is not supposed to be used as a punishment, but couples can get less generous about who does what when each is feeling stressed, underappreciated, or overwhelmed. No marriage benefits from a rigid quid pro quo; the old cliché about everyone doing more than 50 percent is on target. Staying away from a bookkeeper's mentality is important but harder to do than couples think it will be.

Relationship Redundancy

This brings up a cost in efficiency. Equality causes redundancy. Sometimes there are start-up costs: the father has to learn how to handle the baby, talk to the stepchild, or not retreat to the role of disciplinarian. If both partners are at the PTA meeting, no one is attending to other important household or personal responsibilities. The new family economists say that this inefficiency doesn't make sense, and won't make couples happy. They do not seem to be right for this sample of couples—but that doesn't mean some couples won't be upset and negatively affected by the obvious inefficiencies of their collaboration.

Role Discomfort

There is the problem of hating to do jobs firmly situated in the role traditions of the other sex. Most of the couples I interviewed had some little cache of traditionalism they couldn't bear to disturb. Few women tinkered with their car; few men did mending (although one near-peer husband, who seemed to be longing to be in a peer relationship but was kept from it by the impossible hours and consuming nature of his work—and by a wife who claimed the children as her own—adored sewing and made almost all of his children's clothes). Learning an unfamiliar skill is unpleasant to many people, and some never feel good about it. Couples have to figure out which traditional jobs can stay in the traditional sex's repertoire and which have to be challenged. That's not easy, and if there is strong disagreement, it causes conflict since the equity as well as the equality rule is violated.

Competition

Replication makes it easier for each partner to compare himself or herself to the other and risks the possibility of competition—a competitiveness that traditional couples avoid by operating in different realms. The couple has to work at understanding that each person is doing as well as he or she can—and that helps the whole rather than makes one person less adequate. This is another challenge to each person's level of maturity and ego security.

The Emotional and Sexual Costs of a Leaderless Relationship

There are other costs of not having a division of labor with veto power by one person. While the need to negotiate builds respect, a consensus model takes more time, and it can be wearing to have to take responsibility for a bit of everything in the relationship. The lack of a clear leader or of nonoverlapping areas of control means that some things can fall through the cracks because each person assumes the other will bring them up or take care of them. This happens in peer sexual relationships because initiation is designated as both partners' responsibility. If each person thinks it is time for the other person to take the lead, nothing happens. If they are both stewing over the fact that no sex is going on, resentment builds up because each feels the other is shirking responsibility, and this can also be coded as disinterest or selfishness. Interpretations of behaviors based on traditional atributes of men and women still lurk in everyone's heart, and a woman who is not being asked for sex enough may feel deeply insulted because she still feels he should be more interested or more active than she is—even if they are supposed to be equally in charge of their sex life. If the woman has not gotten over women's disinclination to be the aggressive sexual partner but still doesn't want the relationship to operate in sexually traditional ways, the result is that sexual intimacy is going to happen less and sexual contact will be embroiled in a subtle but real power struggle. This mix of new agendas and old inhibitions or expectations can be a problem in other areas as well—everything from putting the couple's social life together to who is supposed to make the next romantic gesture.

Sexual Disinterest

The orchestration of sexual intimacy is a touchy area. For a few, there is the creation of something very much like an incest taboo. Sex may suffer if the "best friend" identity of a spouse overwhelms the identity of lover. The anxiety, the wish to please, and even the hierarchy of traditional and near-peer marriages can create a sexual charge. Sex traditionally can be a main mode of intimacy—the main way to conquer the gap between men and women. Peer couples, without the same gap, have few of these kinds of tensions. Less emotionally needy, they have to be careful that their sex life does not become infrequent. While almost all couples watch the intensity of their sex life diminish over time, getting used to a cozier, friendlier kind of sex is hard for younger couples. Peer couples have to be more imaginative than most, in order to shuck off the "best friend" identity, temporarily, if they want their sex life to be passionate. Not paying attention to this part of their life makes them vulnerable for an affair or a loss of physical intimacy.

Conflict over Parenting Philosophies

Of course, there are challenges brought on by coparenting. Coparenting requires skillful cooperation. It is very satisfying as long as the couple comes up with a mutually satisfactory theory of child development, education, discipline, and reward. If the partners have different philosophies of child raising, the need for close collaboration—and the inability of one person to pull rank and just decide what is going to happen—offers room for conflict. In that case, coparenting can be a major source of dissatisfaction in the relationship, and a lot of time will have to be invested in working out a mutually desirable philosophy. Since both parents are heavily invested in the parenting role, such disagreements are serious for the relationship.

Social Disapproval

In all of the changes that peer couples have taken on, there is the continuing cost of skepticism or criticism from a large number of other people who feel that male participation in traditional female spheres is inappropriate and a dereliction of duty by both partners. These dissenting voices can cause pain, and doubt. One couple interviewed said they no longer went to family holiday gatherings because the disapproval from relatives was more than they could handle.

Over time, many of these costs go away, and challenges get met and solved. Old habits are less familiar, and new roles work more fluidly. But in the beginning or during times of stress (for example, when an adolescent child gets in trouble or aging parents demand attention and resources), the struggle to keep things fair and equal is tiring and sometimes alienating. Still, as these couples' stories have demonstrated, the rewards are great. Men live women's lives with them, and the end of separate spheres means a considerable advance of intimacy and respect. Children profit enormously. They get to know their father better, they get his attention, and they are more likely to have his commitment, regardless of whether the marriage survives.

Yet surely the new attachment to children's everyday lives is an added inducement to marital stability. Women value men who are engaged and committed fathers. Men are relieved of their lonely job of taking total responsibility for life-style and leadership. Their wife is either an earner or a manager and an equal part of their family financial effort. Spouses understand each other better. Granted, not every man wants this partnership, this engagement with children, this modification of his traditional role. But judging from the older men in this sample who came to a peer philosophy later in life, there are more men who have the potential for this kind of partnership than do it. Some of them never get asked to be in an equal relationship; some of them slip away into the throes of work and providing; others never imagine that it is possible to modify work to accommodate parenting.

Given how hard it is to put this all together and the real costs that exist to dissuade people when things get difficult, it seems appropriate to end this book with some of the practical suggestions that peer couples have used to form and maintain their marriages.

Strategies for Creating and Maintaining a Peer Marriage

I am a sociologist and not a therapist, so it will fall to some other writer to give a discussion of the psychological profile a peer spouse might have or the interpersonal exercises that might help each partner understand the other's needs. But given that I think there are men and women ready for peer marriage who simply need to be convinced that it is possible—and understand what undermines it—I will keep my suggestions practical. The suggestions that follow are less my own than what I have derived from my interviews, and from the additional peer couples I meet serendipitously almost every week when I tell people about the study and book I have been working on. Of course, I cannot help but throw in a few insights from my own marriage.

The Job

Examine job plans carefully. There should be a theory about how the job will fit with a personal life and what are reasonable modifications that could make the job fit a peer life-style—as well as which jobs will resist peer values ferociously.

Both jobs need to be flexible—if not at first, then eventually. (Eventually cannot mean twenty years; it means no more than a few years of what you think the relationship can sustain without falling hoplessly into patterns that will undermine intent.)

Applicants do not need to be straightforward with employers right away (going on a job interview and saying that your family will come first is not a good strategy). Being an excellent worker will keep you employed and promoted even if you spend most of your free time at home with your family. The proof of your ability to have a strong commitment to home as well as work is best demonstrated by showing that it can be done.

But some jobs just can't work—not unless you want to be a crusader. In practical terms peer marriage means no jobs where being in the office all the time is requisite to show company loyalty. Nor does it mean jobs that take you away from home all the time or at unpredictable times that you can never control; jobs that snarl at family leave for family as well as personal crises; jobs in which other people's schedules can always dictate your own. Jobs you can control by project, jobs done at home, jobs where you can change your schedule weekly or quarterly, or jobs where you are your own employer give more chance to craft a personal fit of work and family. Another alternative is to have a high-powered job that you can control and rewards getting the job done through independence of action rather than punching a time clock. Jobs that require sacrifice for a training period but then allow latitude and personal control of time are fine.

Partners should try to find jobs that are in sync. Increasingly, couples meet when they are older and established in some kind of work. We marry later in life and often fall in love with someone who has different job constraints. Musicians have to have a certain number of hours to practice, and they have night and weekend performances. Many of them are married to other musicians; when they aren't, the rigors of practice and performance may cause conflict. On the other hand, a musician might become a teacher or change his or her career so that there is not constant touring or massive amounts of practice that take away from the ability to build a family. Most careers have more latitude than one might think.

Most important is to be honest about what the job means and what is necessary for personal fulfillment. The couples in this book leveled with one another and could work out mutually agreeable solutions. Too many women have stifled their ambitions, only to find themselves choking on regrets. Each partner has to be honest about how much work they want to do and how they want to do it. Then negotiation is possible.

The couple needs to keep in mind that money cannot be the core dimension that orients their choices. Both partners might want to work hard so that they can live a good life —but if the time together is lost for too long, the possibility of a deep friendship is lost too. Keeping track of what the jobs are doing for or to the marriage and family is a necessary exercise for all workers, from the litigator in court for three months to the factory worker who keeps signing up for overtime.

Money

No one person should feel economically dependent on the other. The larger resources should be pooled. But people should also have some private money so that neither party always has to come to the other for economic largesse. It is the mix of interdependence and privacy that allows each person to feel good about money.

Women are usually the lower earner. If salaries are matched and other personal resources are similar, no one partner should feel economically dominated. But when the woman earns less, it is important that resources be shared legally, practically, and ideologically. If there is a great deal of difference in incomes, it may be necessary to create a fund for the wife that makes her feel more economically independent. There should not be two social classes within the same marriage. If there are reasons that property needs to be kept separate, then a new fund needs to be created that profits and is controlled by both partners. Without some system of financial equity, the peer model is very hard to achieve.

Planning and Goal Setting

Mutual goals need to be created whereby individual success profits the whole. Some couples work together; others use present individual success for a joint payoff. That could mean planning early retirement and a family trip for a year; a joint commitment to charitable endeavors and service with the fame or money that one of the person makes; a life plan of building a house or get-away or a stake for old age. The point is that some of each person's success needs to be couple success too. A deep sense of corporate accomplishment should make each partner proud of the other; there needs to be a joint project that makes success rewarding to the less directly rewarded partner.

A Network of Other Peers

People don't often talk about the basis of their relationship, and they may miss chances to find out that there are others around like themselves. When I would talk about this book informally, people would rather shyly or proudly say, "You know, I have a marriage like that."

Everyone needs support now and then for the way they live, and seeking out other like-minded couples is important.

The Parental Front

Children know what a mother is supposed to look and act like, and they will want their mother to look and act that way. They will generally welcome father involvement, but both parents will have to work to convince their children that father involvement is not a poor substitute for mother presence. Peer couples constantly said they had to work hardest against playing roles true to stereotype—father as disciplinarian, mother as comforter. Each parent has to be valuable to the child under a variety of circumstances. Of course, there will always be different talents and varying amounts of patience or playfulness, but peer couples advise playing against narrow roles as much as possible. Children need to be queried (particularly older ones) about how parents are doing and whether collaborations are perceived as intended.

Peer spouses also advise introducing both parents to the children's teachers early in the school year and complain to the school or faculty if they start to rely totally or principally on the mother. Many couples warned against letting teachers give de facto senior parenting status to the mother. If fathers aren't included, they make a big deal if it. These are not just symbolic acts but socialization needed to support the theory of the relationship.

Friendship

Peer spouses find that the best guide to relationship enhancement is keeping platonic friendship in mind. Treating the spouse no worse than a best friend has a continually civilizing effect, even if it only helps to clarify when an apology is necessary.

One way to monitor the relationship is to notice conversational styles in the relationship. An egalitarian relationship allows each partner a similar amount of speaking time, a similar number of interruptions, a similar amount of supportive work in conversation, and a negotiating rather than preemptive or officious or presumptive style. Anything else should be noted, discussed, and changed.

Couples advise against the seduction of leaving most of one's interesting stories and feelings from work at the workplace. It is easy to get so much satisfying exchange from colleagues that there is no incentive to bring the information home. The challenge is not to live separate and parallel lives.

Household Tasks

It is hard to imagine how many household jobs there really are. Certainly there are enough to keep one person busy doing just household labor from sunup to sundown. Most people solve that dilemma by ignoring some household needs, delaying them as long as possible, settling for imperfect cleaning and projects, or hiring outside help. If hiring isn't an option—or even if it is—there are always going to be many jobs to do.

Sometimes women end up doing them because it feels simpler just to do the job oneself. Coordinating and explaining and training seem too much to contemplate. But it is important to resist that impulse and spend the time to figure out a system about how to divide up chores. That division of labor should also include household management. Planning and cleaning together is part of building team consciousness and empathy.

Sexual Intimacy

Sex has to be taken on as a project because friendship has the capacity to overpower the erotic themes of the relationship. Peer couples do not need sex for intimacy, but they do need it for romance. Adult getaways or weekends provide the staging for eroticism. This may seem artificial to partners who are so open and familiar to one another; nonetheless, peers recommend the creation of a separate sexual sphere.

This can be done by making the bedroom sensual, off limits to children, and shop talk or by allowing a different self to emerge in bed—a self that has nothing to do with being a mother, father, or friend. The more different that self is, the more passionate the couple's sexual life is likely to be, at least from time to time. However, coming to terms with the fact that habituation modifies sexual need is probably necessary. There is no need to give up on passion, but sex as an expression of intimacy and affection is going to be more likely than the fireworks of two people who can only surmount the distance between them in a heightened passionate state. The challenge for peer couples is to shake up their sexual relationship every now and then and not let sex get so friendly that it never allows for another self to emerge and excite the other person. Peer couples will naturally have warm and friendly sex. What they need to work on is psychic experimentation. To some extent, this may be more possible than in conventional relationships since no role behaviors are forbidden to either spouse.

In Sum

There are no rules on how to construct a peer marriage. For the couples interviewed for this book, the impetus usually came from a rejection of past experience—a woman who demanded equality of her spouse, or a man who was searching to make his wife and children the center of his life. But there are idiosyncratic routes to the same place, and people are able to change over the lifecycle from one kind of marriage to another. Age seems to tame men's preoccupation with work and control, and it gives women more courage, self-confidence, and direction. Some couples will develop peer marriages only in the senior segment of their lives. It is a strong argument for "better late than never."

But there is no need for anyone to wait. Peer marriage respects the potential of each person and gives men and women a chance to overcome the biology and sociology that separate them. Future generations might be renewed by a powerful new phase of marriage: two people who can create a strong and durable family because their relationship is secured by a commitment to equality that is underwritten by a deep and abiding friendship.

Notes

CHAPTER 1: THE HARD EXPERIENCE OF EQUALITY

1. Philip Blumstein and Pepper Schwartz, *American Couples* (New York: William Morrow, 1983).
2. Arlie Hochschild with A. Machung, *The Second Shift* (New York: Viking, 1989).
3. Philip Blumstein and Pepper Schwartz, *American Couples*. See also Philip Blumstein and Pepper Schwartz, "Money and Ideology: Their Impact on Power and the Division of Household Labor," and Judith Treas, "The Common Pot or Separate Purses? A Transactional Analysis," both in Rae Lesser Blumber, Ed., *Gender, Family and Economy* (Newbury Park, Calif.: Sage, 1991).

CHAPTER 2: DEEP FRIENDSHIP

1. Associated Press. "Who Do You Want To Be On An Island With?" *Seattle Times*, June 1993.
2. Judith Howard, Philip Blumstein, and Pepper Schwartz, "Sex, Power and Influence Tactics in Intimate Relationships," *Journal of Personality and Social Behavior* 51, No. 1 (1986).
3. Deborah Tannen, *That's Not What I Meant!* (New York: William Morrow, 1986).
4. Howard, Blumstein, and Schwartz, "Sex, Power and Influence Tactics in Intimate Relationships."
5. Ibid.
6. Francesca Cancian, *Love In America: Gender and Self Development* (New York: Cambridge University Press, 1987).
7. Barbara Risman, "Can Men Mother?" *Family Relations*, Vol. 35 (1986).

CHAPTER 3: PASSION IN A SEXUAL DEMOCRACY

1. Philip Blumstein and Pepper Schwartz, *American Couples*.
2. Alan Bloom, "The Death of Eros," *New York Times Magazine*, May 23, 1993.
3. David Schnarsh, *Constructing the Sexual Crucible* (New York: Norton, 1991).

4. E. Hatfield and R. Rapson, *Love, Sex and Intimacy* (New York: Harper Collins College, 1993), p. 92.
5. William H. Masters and Virginia E. Johnson, *Human Sexual Response* (Boston: Little Brown, 1966).
6. M. Brown and A. Auerbach, "Communication Patterns in Initiation of Marital Sex," *Medical Aspects of Human Sexuality*. 15, pp. 107–117. 1981.
7. E. Berscheid, *"Emotion,"* In H. H. Kelly, E. Berscheid, A. Christensen, J. H. Harvey, T. L. Huston, G. Levinger, E. McClintock, L. A. Peplau and D.R. Peterson, Eds., *Close Relationships* (New York: Freeman, 1983), pp. 110–168. Also Sternberg, R. J. "Triangulating Love." In R. J. Sternberg and M. L. Barnes, Eds., *The Psychology of Love* (New Haven: Yale University Press) pp. 119–138.
8. D. Dutton and A. Aron, "Some evidence for heightened sexual attraction under conditions of high anxiety," *Journal of Personality and Social Psychology*, Vol. 30 (1974), pp. 510–517.
9. Andrea Dworking, *Intercourse* (New York, NY: Free Press, 1987).
10. Blumstein and Schwartz, *American Couples*.
11. L. Atwater, *The Extramarital Connection: Sex, Intimacy and Identity* (New York: Irvington, 1982). Also Andrew Greeley, *The Fidelity Epidemic: A Report on Intimacy and Love in American Marriage* (New York: Psychology Today Book, 1991).
12. Martin King Whyte, *Dating, Mating and Marriage* (New York: Aldine de Gruyter, 1990), pp. 25–27, 381–387, 247–253.
13. Annette Lawson, *Adultery: An Analysis of Love and Betrayal* (New York: Basic Books, 1988).
14. Andrew Greeley, *The Fidelity Epidemic*.
15. Blumstein and Schwartz, *American Couples*.

CHAPTER 4:   ELIMINATING THE PROVIDER ROLE

1. Blumstein and Schwartz, *American Couples*.
2. Marsha Millman, *Warm Hearts and Cold Cash* (New York: The Free Press, 1991); Jan Pahl, *Money and Marriage* (New York: St. Martin's Press, 1989).
3. Jan Pahl, *Money and Marriage*.
4. Philip Blumstein and Pepper Schwartz, "Money and Ideology: Their Impact on Power and the Division of Household Labor," in Rae Lesser Blumberg, Ed., *Gender, Family and Economy* (Newbury Park, Calif.: Sage, 1991).
5. Jan Pahl, *Money and Marriage*.
6. Blumstein and Schwartz, *American Couples;* also Judith Treas, "Transaction Costs and the Economic Organization of Marriage," *American Sociological Review*, Vol. 58, No. 5 (Oct. 1993), pp. 723–734.
7. Sue Sprecher and Pepper Schwartz, "Equity and Balance in the Exchange of Contributions in Close Relationships," in Melvin Lerner and

Gerald Mikula, *Entitlement and the Affectional Bond* (New York: Plenum, 1993).

8. P. England, and G. Farkas, *Households, Employment, and Gender: A Social, Economic and Demographic View* (New York: Aldine de Gruyter, 1986). Also: Janice Steel and Karen Weltman, "Marital Inequality: The Importance of Resources, Personal Attributes and Social Norms on Career Valuing and the Allocation of Domestic Responsibilities." *Sex Roles Journal*, Vol. 24, No. 314 (1991). Also Philip Blumstein and Pepper Schwartz, "Money and Ideology: Their Impact on Power and the Division of Household Labor." in Rae Lesser Blumberg, Ed., *Gender, Family and Economy* (Newbury Park, Calif.: Sage, 1991).

9. "Sexual Static," in *Health Care Forum* (Health Care Forum, May–June 1987), pp. 25–30.

10. Blumstein and Schwartz, *American Couples*.

11. Julie Brines, "Gender, Economic Dependence and the Division of Labor at Home," *American Journal of Sociology*, forthcoming, 1994; also "The Exchange Value of Housework," *Rationality and Society*, Vol. 5 (1993), pp. 302–340; also Julie Brines and Karen Joyner "The Ties That Bind: Principles of Stability in the Modern Union," manuscript under review, 1994.

CHAPTER 5: THE SHARED CHILD

1. Angus Campbell, Philip Converse, and Willard Rogers, *The Quality of American Life* (New York: Russell Sage, 1976). Also Martin King Whyte, *Dating, Mating and Marriage* (New York: Aldine de Gruyter, 1990). Also B. C. Rollins, and K. L., Cannon, "Marital Satisfaction Over The Family Life Cycle: A reevaluation," *Journal of Marriage and the Family*, Vol. 36 (1974) pp. 271–283.

2. Jay Belsky, "Children in Marriage," in F. D. Fincham and T. N. Bradbury, Eds., *The Psychology of Marriage: Basic Issues and Applications* (New York: Guilford Press), pp. 172–200. Also J.H. Block, J. Block, and J. Morrison, "Parental agreement-disagreement on child rearing orientations and gender-related personality correlates in children." *Child Development*, Vol. 52, pp. 965–974. Also L. Steinberg, "The Impact of Puberty on Family Relations," *Developmental Psychology*, Vol. 23, pp. 451–460.

3. Diane Lye, "Where's Daddy? Paternal Participation in Childraising in Intact Families." Paper presented at the Annual Meetings of the Population Association of America, Washington, D.C., Mar 21–23, 1991. Also Morgan S. Philip, Diane Lye, and Gretchen A. Condran, "Sons, Daughters and Marital Disruption," *American Journal of Sociology* (1991).

4. Gary Becker, *Treatise on the Family* (Cambridge, MA: Harvard University Press, 1991).

5. Blumstein and Schwartz, *American Couples*.

6. Andrew Cherlin, *Marriage, Divorce, Remarriage* (Cambridge, MA: Harvard University Press, 1992), especially Chapter 3.

7. Andrew Cherlin, "Remarriage as an Incomplete Institution," *American Journal of Sociology*, 84 (Nov 1978), pp. 634–650.

CHAPTER 6:   THE FUTURE OF PEER MARRIAGE

1. Charles Vert Willie, *A New Look at Black Families*, 3d ed. (New York: General Hall Publishers, 1988), especially Chapter 4; also Robert Staples, *The Black Family*, 5th ed. (Belmont, CA: Wadsworth, 1993), especially Sections 5 and 6.

Index